Industry Week's
Guide to
Tomorrow's Executive:

Humanagement
in the Future
Corporation

Industry Week's Guide to Tomorrow's Executive:

Humanagement in the Future Corporation

Perry Pascarella

Foreword by **Stanley J. Modic**

VNR VAN NOSTRAND REINHOLD COMPANY
NEW YORK   CINCINNATI   ATLANTA   DALLAS   SAN FRANCISCO
LONDON   TORONTO   MELBOURNE

Van Nostrand Reinhold Company Regional Offices:
New York   Cincinnati   Atlanta   Dallas   San Francisco

Van Nostrand Reinhold Company International Offices:
London   Toronto   Melbourne

Manufactured in the United States of America

Published simultaneously in Canada by Van Nostrand Reinhold Ltd.

15 14 13 12 11 10 9 8 7 6 5 4 3 2

Library of Congress Cataloging in Publication Data

Pascarella, Perry.
   Industry Week's guide to tomorrow's executive: humanagement in the future corporation.

   Includes bibliographical references and index.
   1. Management. I.   Industry week.   II. Title.
HD31.P315   658.4   80-12879
ISBN 0-442-23122-9

*To the managers of yesterday, who helped us realize our dreams,
and the managers of tomorrow, with whom we dream new dreams.*

Foreword

For more than a decade, the editors of *Industry Week* have been dealing with management as a profession. Through tens of thousands of interviews and dozens of surveys, seminars, and conferences with the people that make business go, we have explored the problems that management faces. Our studies and probing have focused heavily on the executive's two principal concerns — the management of people and their own needs as individuals. We have delved deeply into what makes corporations run: "people relationships."

There are many books available on management principles, on the corporate structure, on how to get ahead in business. We have read many of them. But there is more to successful managing than principle and theory. The role of management is to put money, machinery, and material together by working through people to obtain objectives. People are the most variable ingredient in the management mix, exerting great influence through their contribution to the organization and in their demands upon it. Thus, we saw the need for a book that brings together the changes in people and in organizations that are affecting the role of management.

The sweeping social changes that are affecting corporations and the shifting values of managers in their approach to their work are not taking place in separate worlds. They are intertwined. We saw the need to discuss the changes in the public's attitude toward the corporation, the workers' attitude toward their work, and the managers' attitude toward their assignment. Separately, any of these changes could destroy the corporate structure as we know it today.

We think that through "Humanagement," they will blend together to reshape the corporation of tomorrow to make it more responsive to society, economically more productive, and a better place to work.

Humanagement is not based on wishful thinking but rather on a hard look at today's reality. Some will construe it as a soft approach. What it really suggests is a higher form of management — one that is much harder, not easier, to effect.

Organizations are what people make them. Much attention has been given to the forces outside the business structure calling for change. And yet one of the greatest forces reshaping our organizations is being applied from within, from the executives and managers as they express their personal wants and needs. The changes we foresee will challenge many of the fundamental assumptions on which corporate management and personal executive advancement have been based.

It is not a palace revolution as much as it is a coming of age for a new generation of management. One that will be different. One that managers and executives alike will have to master in order to survive.

Stanley J. Modic
Editor, *Industry Week*

Preface

Laying out issue after issue of a magazine, editors knowingly or unknowingly build something. Their rows of brick become steps leading somewhere.

In the ten years of *Industry Week's* history, I have worked with numerous fellow editors. Our purpose has constantly been to help corporate executives perform better in their jobs — and, more than that, to perform the right jobs. We have done this not by looking backward, but by looking forward. We have kept in mind certain assumptions about the corporate role and the executive's role in the corporation. As we enter the 1980's and as *Industry Week* celebrates its tenth anniversary, we take this opportunity to show where our stairway is headed.

Thanks go to Publisher Patrick Keefe and Editor Stan Modic for giving me carte blanche to write as I saw fit; to my *Industry Week* colleagues, whose articles I have raided for quotes and examples — the bricks of our stairway; and to Geri Baran for her miles of typing through each draft of this book's manuscript.

Not until I had nearly finished writing did I realize how much of what I'd presented here had been influenced by the thinking of Frederick Herzberg, distinguished professor of management at the University of Utah, and a contributing editor to *Industry Week*. We have worked together on two dozen articles over the past ten years; our many discussions of man and management have helped me immeasurably in knowing which bricks to select and where to place them.

While I am aware that there are many women in management today and many more aspiring to enter the ranks of management, I have generally — but not always — used the third person, masculine pronoun in this book. I do not feel that the use of "he or she," "his and her," or "him/herself" would make for greater clarity, better reading, or a faster rise of women in our organizations.

Perry Pascarella
Executive Editor, *Industry Week*

Contents

Industry Week's
Guide to
Tomorrow's Executive:

Humanagement
in the Future
Corporation

1
The Humanization of Management

The people who have managed American business developed an arsenal of skills that have made the U.S. system a world giant in the generation of wealth. But this economic success has fostered a society which now clamors for changes in its economic goals and for the satisfaction of non-economic needs. Because it has proven to be a successful vehicle for delivering the goods, the business corporation is being challenged to deliver solutions on a far broader scale.

This turning point in corporate history necessitates a change in attitudes and style for those who exercise those management skills. It suggests, perhaps, that the business executive's role will take on "superhuman" dimensions.

New objectives for the corporation are not being laid down in a rational, cohesive pattern. The expectations levied on today's corporations take executives into areas which were traditionally of secondary concern, or of no concern at all, in terms of getting their jobs done. Economic and social objectives are being dictated to the corporation in such detail and with such speed that it seems impossible to attain any of them. They jeopardize the life of the corporation.

Response to these demands calls for remarkably capable people to fill the ranks of management. The ideal manager of the future will have to be quite different from his or her predecessors. The new manager will have to be sensitive to shifting demands and answerable to new constituencies.

The challenge from without, however, may be offset by a challenge from within; that is, the need for a more humanistic corporation may be offset by the changes in what managers themselves want to invest in their work and what they want to derive from it. They, too, will press for change. The external and internal forces, then, may hold the corporation together so that it can fulfill its broader role.

What appears to be a job for superhuman executives may be quite the contrary. The managerial role is not growing beyond the abilities of man, but is *expanding to* the human scale. It calls upon people to unleash more of their talents and realize more of their humanness. The manager who would not allow himself to be crammed into corporate boxes will find that those boxes are collapsing.

The corporation will change, but not without struggles and imbalances. There is a great deal of built-in resistance to any "capitulation" to demands — whether they be external or internal. But change will come, since an organization has no basis for existence if it becomes irrelevant to the people who comprise it, or to the society which permits it to exist.

The manager will find the job requiring not the accumulation of greater power, but the sharing of power. It will reject loftiness in favor of greatness in human terms. The manager will be able to bring more human capabilities to the job, will be free to admit his or her limitations, and will be less compelled to be confined to limited objectives and be cloaked in a mantle of perfection. A pivotal factor in determining the viability of the future corporation will be the ability of the manager to employ humanity and interpersonal skills to direct the corporation toward new economic and social objectives.

The expectations today's corporations are up against are virtually all based on the assumption that the corporation is a permanent institution. The corporation is expected to provide a form of socialization by insuring income stability, pensions, and health care. It must work toward social objectives by providing equal opportunities for employment, training, and advancement. It must be sensitive to the political ramifications of its dealings with other nations and institutions. As the corporation broadens in terms of its objectives, as well as in terms of its ownership base and geographic reach, it becomes a public instrument.

Not only corporate objectives but the means by which they are pursued are subject to challenge today. Inside the company, workers want more than a day's pay for doing what they're told to do. They want rewarding work, a sense of community, and an opportunity to participate in the decisions that affect them. Outside the company, countless individuals and groups employ various tactics for shaping the ends and the means of corporate activity.

No matter how many objectives are added to the corporate role, there is no escaping the economic imperative: compete or perish. In fact, the advance of economic powers elsewhere in the world heightens the necessity to improve productivity and generate innovation — an awesome challenge in light of the social objectives that add to costs and divert management attention.

The assumption of corporate permanence is unjustified. The business corporation is a relatively new form of organization, initiated to bring capital together and to limit the obligations (financial and otherwise) of the stockholders. Thousands of corporations are formed every year and thousands go out of business; some do not even make it through the first year. As the corporation becomes the focal point for the disharmony of conflicting needs and wants, "success" by anyone's standards won't come easily. As success in one pursuit detracts from success in another, there should be little wonder that the corporation is falling short of expectations.

Some managers regard the pressures on the corporation as an attempt to destroy the private enterprise system. But surveys show again and again that most Americans have a high regard for the system. They are, however, not satisfied with the performance of those who operate the system. Their expectations have been elevated and they express their confidence in the system by turning to the corporation to provide them what they want. Since the corporation has generally not taken the initiative in satisfying each of these demands, individuals and groups prod the corporation. The more they prod, the more they hobble the corporation with conflicting demands, and thus the more they have to prod.

This pushing and resisting intensifies the public's impression that the corporation lacks the soul required to take a leadership position. It reaffirms the notion that managers may not be competent to manage our institutions, since they have, after all, concentrated on the financial or technical aspects of running a business.

New measurements of corporate success (or signs of relevance) are now being considered in human terms. The individual who enjoys a base of economic security looks for ways to find self-fulfillment and meaning in his or her life. Unfortunately, the individual may see the corporation as a faceless, inhumane monolith which is not interested in human values, safety, or the well being of the planet. The question, then, is whether corporate growth is a measure of success; the individual doubts that hierarchical structures can bring forth the best solutions (or even treat the right problems) where people's values are concerned.

The corporate manager likes to think of himself as an agent of change. But change, up to now, has been limited to playing by the economic rules to succeed in economic terms. The manager is now faced with fundamental change in the definition of what is to be done and how. He or she has two alternatives: to resist the demands and hope to turn back the tide of change, or to welcome the added challenges and see in them hope for a better personal future.

TRADITIONAL CONFLICTS

People outside the corporation may hold little hope that any change in the right direction will come from within. This country has thrived on adversary relationships, and the manager/non-manager feud is a favorite. Many people are not sure what a manager really is (or does), but they have an endless supply of terms for managers — "big shot," "fat cat," "big cheese," "wheeler-dealer." Most of the terms and images fall short of being complimentary, to say the least. They tend to set managers off from "the rest of us."

Putting on the coat and tie of management seals off an individual's humanity, many people are convinced. The ten million Americans who hold managerial or administrative positions in private business and government must accept the traditional condemnation of being a cog in the system's heartless machinery.

These images do not serve us well. They color all managers the same lifeless shade. For every wheeler-dealer or fat cat, there are many managers who get the goods produced and still serve the community. While some managers may be detached from the outside world, there are thousands playing key roles on the boards of schools, hospitals, and churches. Business executives head Boy Scout fund raising drives, and thousands of managers lead troops on camp-outs or coach little leaguers.

Because of the power that goes with being a manager − and because of remembrances of what that power once was − it's natural for a manager/non-manager power struggle to exist. After all, a manager can hire and fire, determine how much a worker will be paid, and decide what the worker will do, as well as where and when it will be done. The worker continually tries to whittle away at this power, attempting to gain more control over his or her own life.

In varying degrees, the manager has been separated not only from others but also from his or her own emotions and personal values, and from the morality of society. These things have traditionally been irrelevant to fulfilling the corporate role. In exchange, the manager was able to derive a sense of belonging and identity from the organization. But this Faustian bargain does not have the appeal it once did.

The changing role of business may be relatively easy to observe. Less obvious, however, is the change in the managerial role that is likely to be demanded by managers themselves. The manager shares in the social changes taking place − driven not only by society's rising expectations, but by personal expectations, as well. The manager's own expectations of the job, of life, and of the corporation are changing. A broader range of objectives and new techniques for managing are welcomed.

The new breed (of all ages) sees the opportunity to find more meaningful work and lead a more integrated life. Today, a manager may take a much broader view in the search for identity. The identity derived from position or company affiliation is too confining, and today's manager shares in the exploration of new values. The new ideology may go beyond a simple *laissez faire* attitude, with the manager relating himself *and* the organization to the rest of the world and its needs. The manager needs something to believe in beyond the traditional job accomplishments. What he does, how, and with whom — as well as how what is done relates to the manager's whole life — have become important considerations.

Management is adopting a highly experimental stance for three reasons. First, organizations are swamped by the demands being thrust at them. Second, productivity improvement is not adequate to offset inflation or to beat foreign competitors. Third, managers themselves are bringing new perspectives to their work. Increasingly, they reject the model of single-minded individuals for whom profit or product is be-all and the end-all. Because many of today's managers demand satisfying work and the opportunity to achieve, they can appreciate others' longing for the same things. They are experimenting with new methods of communicating, decision-making, and working together. Lateral relationships repeatedly show that they can work better than militaristic hierarchy and often produce better informed decisions and better follow-through.

CHALLENGE AND ACHIEVEMENT

The corporation of the future will be shaped by the people who manage it as well as by external pressures. As managers express their need to achieve in broader terms than in the past, they will come closer to harmonizing with the world outside. Middle management and professional people want "more interesting and vital work and more of a chance to find a commitment they deem worthy of their talents and skills." says social analyst Daniel Yankelovich, President of Yankelovich, Skelly & White, Inc., a public opinion research firm. He places about one out of six workers in this college educated, whitecollar category. They are the "most willing to sacrifice either money or job security in order to fulfill these needs."

For some managers, work is not only fulfilling — it is exciting. Strapped and wired into a flight simulator for the space shuttle, George W. Jeffs, vice president of Rockwell International Corp., and president of its North American space operations, checked progress on the construction of the vehicle designed to make repeated trips into space. Speaking of the project he was captaining, the graying, 52-year-old executive said: "We put the reputation of our company, of ourselves personally, our organizations, our people on the line every time we do something that is significant. The rewards for this are certainly not in the profits. Our profits, compared with those of commercial industry, are probably about half — at best. The thing that we're most concerned about is the success that we want to see out of our efforts. We're all in it to make a living, of course, but I think, fundamentally, that we're in it for the satisfaction of doing something different, something that hasn't been done before," says Mr. Jeffs.

Effective managers are driven by the desire to achieve — but in a special way. Unlike other achievers, they want to perform work through others. The scale of what they want to accomplish is such that they cannot work alone. It's the difference between a violinist and a conductor. Both are achievers. Both are highly motivated by their work. Both have talent — but different talents. To over-simplify, one makes sounds; the other waves his arms. If we see a manager only in terms of waving his arms, we might question his contribution. But if we look deeper to see him interpret, direct, and coordinate, we can appreciate his role.

Unfortunately, not all managers are effective. Many are not really managers. Some are "maintenance experts" — not inclined to pursue change. Some got where they are because they were the best in their specialty, and management picked them to manage others. Although a different set of skills is required to manage, as opposed to being a good engineer or a good accountant, people have sought (or, at least, accepted) promotions into management in order to earn a better salary or enhance their status. There are those, too, who resent anyone who tries to rock the boat, preferr-ing to do little more than the minimum for survival; in their con-cern for protecting themselves they may even be hostile to the organization.

In traditional corporate structures, power and authority go with certain positions. They are the tools for getting things done. But, for some managers, power is an end in itself. Ralph may want to be vice president of his company, not because he wants to guide it into new markets, meet social needs, or improve the profit po-sition, but because he wants more pay, more recognition, more people reporting to him, or fewer bosses to report to. His wife may want to be president of the P.T.A., not because she wants to improve the quality of education, but because she wants people to admire her.

There are wheeler-dealers in the management ranks, too. They concentrate on stocks, bonds, tender offers, and proxy fights, moving companies in a bigger-than-life chess game. Unfortunately, these people — along with those who are just struggling to hang onto their positions — make the best material for novels and movies. The image they project obscures those managers who actually get the work done — the work that gives stocks their value and makes companies worth fighting for.

Sometimes even these producers can get too caught up in short-term, narrowly defined objectives. They unintentionally become allies with the power grabbers, status quo protectors, and wheeler-dealers in resisting or ignoring the pressures for change.

The corporation, then, can rely on relatively few members of its management team for adaptation to a changing world. These agents of change continually seek new goals as they attain others. Although they are part of the organization, they are willing to challenge it. They operate by the rules, but they will change rules when old ones get in the way of reaching goals or establishing new goals.

Social analyst Daniel Yankelovich asserts that the middle management group is not finding satisfaction in its work. These people, he says, are the "hungriest for responsibility, challenge, autonomy, informality, and less rigid authority in organization structure." They possess the "strongest creativity and achievement needs" of any workers, but incentive systems based on money and fear don't draw the best from these people, says Mr. Yankelovich. We could extend that line of thinking to justify the need for revising job content and corporate structure.

Even "successful" managers sometimes find that work isn't paying off in terms that are fulfilling to them. They hunger for something in the job besides money or status. Incentives and structures could be changed to give such people what they want and to benefit the corporation by a greater investment of talent. At a time when coercion and artificial enticements aren't effective with the new workforce, the corporation needs managers who can operate with a less precise definition of responsibilities and authority and who can bring people's personal goals into harmony with those of the organization — and vice versa. These managers may bring to the organization both a responsiveness to the outside world and an improvement in productivity.

For better or for worse, managers constitute "the company." Some set company policy and objectives; others implement them. "The company" is the cumulative effect of what they believe and do. The goals they set, the rules they establish, and the tempo and tone with which they operate determine what a company is and how well people like to work for it, buy its products, or own shares of its stock.

Relatively few managers have a big personal stake in the ownership of their company. Gone are the Carnegies and Rockefellers who amassed great fortunes by manipulating investments and people. Today, we have in their places men and women whose income depends on the paycheck and fringe benefits. Taken as a group, corporate executives are barely a minority stockholder in American industry. The chiefs of the giant corporations are not widely known. Outside management and financial circles, neither their names nor their faces draw much recognition.

Management is a relatively new concept. Industry and the organization of work as we know them do not date back to early civilization. The Industrial Revolution of 200 years ago established the general shape of today's business. The manager was the owner. He hired people to work for him, telling them what to do and how to do it. Then came the hired manager to whom the owner delegated specific responsibilities; he learned his craft on the job. Early in this century, some of the skills of engineers and accountants were carried over into management, lending scientific technique to it. Management became increasingly scientific. The human factors were ignored — or deliberately eliminated — in an attempt to quantify everything possible, break jobs down into simple repetitive tasks, and improve efficiency. The early management theorists believed that organizational efficiency rose in proportion to the displacement of individual values with interchangeable functions.

SCOREKEEPING ISN'T THE GAME

Since managers generally don't own the company or even a large percentage of the shares in it, profit doesn't come directly to their pockets. But it does serve as a measurement of their performance. Some are doubly rewarded when they achieve something that they deem worthy in itself and, at the same time, earns a profit for the company. Profit reflects the fact that what you accomplished has value to someone else. The increased value of the company's stock indicates that you have built a wealth-producing organization in which others want to share ownership.

A manager can be carried away by this scorekeeping, however. Many management courses are dedicated to scorekeeping methods, showing the manager how to analyze companies statistically. Certain ratios and relationships help to isolate problems and point out opportunities for improvement. By concentrating too heavily on the numbers, however, a manager may miss the intangibles that are causing a bad situation or may not appreciate some of the positive intangibles that will be disturbed by these efforts to bring the numbers into line for a better score. Watching the scoreboard while ignoring the members of the team, the opponents, and the officials, the manager may lose the game.

Not all managers are in positions where they can measure their performance by profit. But, for nearly all of them, some standard has been set so that they, too, are oriented toward a score such as a sales quota, a production quota, or a cost reduction target.

The standards for measuring a manager's performance are neither universal nor permanent. At times, they may point to maximizing sales growth, or profit growth, or profit as a return on investment, or a gain in the price of the company's stock. At other times, or in other societies, they may emphasize the maintenance of an organization for the long term. They may (and this is increasingly true today in the U.S.) point to serving a variety of society's needs, such as the creation of employment, providing equal opportunities for employment, cleaning up the environment, and conserving resources.

Management functions such as sales, finance, and production — which have a good array of statistical measurements — have been the traditional routes to the top of the corporate hierarchy. The more you could relate your performance to profitability, the greater your chances of making it to the top.

Today, however, most of the problems facing the corporation are beyond measurement. They involve people's values and feelings. The corporate doors and windows have been opened wide, and what was once a private institution has, for all practical purposes, become a public one. Therefore, the corporation deals more and more in people relationships. That is why we have begun to see the rise to prominence of such managerial functions as employee relations, public relations, and government relations. Relations!

In 1977, *Industry Week* magazine recognized this trend when it began its annual series of awards for excellence in management. An outstanding chief executive has been named each year in each of four categories: community relations, government relations, industrial relations, and explaining the private enterprise system to the public. The awards represent a deliberate attempt to draw attention to new yardsticks for performance.

"We were at 12 times earnings; now we're up to 30," says a chief executive. Growth in the ratio of the sales price of his company's stock to its earnings is a source of pride for him. This same manager was a winner of an *Industry Week* award for community relations. The "bottom line" may or may not be his ultimate goal. His success in financial terms is due to more than scientific expertise. His drive for achievement embraces both financial and non-financial objectives. His orientation toward people makes him a success at solving people problems and getting people to help him attain his financial objectives.

Some of the companies that have achieved the best scores are also the most people-oriented (or they have the best scores *because* they are people-oriented). It makes sense. Managers who are concerned with employees' well-being, customers' needs, and the welfare of the public tend to the things that ultimately maximize sales, minimize costs, and generate a good "score."

RECONSTRUCTING WORK

The rules that once worked for attaining financial success are losing their effectiveness today. Early in this century, Taylorism erected a milestone in scientific management. It advocated analyzing jobs and breaking them down into simple, repeatable tasks so as to maximize efficiency. This mechanistic approach to work created machine-like routine for millions of people. The concept fit well into hierarchical structures.

Today, however, industry is trying to undo this approach to work. Because of people's changing expectations, attempts are being made to put jobs back together again. Some managers are trying to reconstruct work in the shape of people. You hear them speak in terms of "job enlargement," "job enrichment," and "humanization of the workplace." They are convinced that better worker relations and improved productivity will have to come through workers' own motivations. They will get more out of people, they figure, by letting workers put more of themselves into the job.

Today, we see a broad spectrum of people-orientation – and the lack of it. There are organizations in which genuine concern for the humanity of people is fundamental to the management style. There are others where the worker is regarded strictly as someone to perform a task. Between these extremes, there is a span of paternalism where management mimics the humanistic approach either because it gets a warm feeling from treating people reasonably or because it hopes to produce an obligation to reciprocate with hard work.

The genuinely humanistic style of management begins with the attempt to understand what people want. Both workers and managers yearn for a better work situation, more freedom in the workplace, and a greater say in decisions that affect their jobs. This is not a revolution brought about by the so-called younger generation. The trend has swept up people of all ages and positions. At the same time, the lack of opportunity to find rewarding work situations has turned off many workers. They haven't lost the will to work, but neither are they interested in accepting work as it has been packaged nor in making personal sacrifices as a term of employment. They express their frustration through demands for more time off, better pay, or other means of compensating for work that is not meaningful to them.

Critics of workplace humanization efforts say these attempts are merely new tactics for manipulating people to keep them in the hierarchy. Their accusations are partly right. Some managers are genuinely interested in people *per se,* and their humanization efforts aim at establishing jobs and relationships that provide meaningful, inner rewards. But others twist the concept into a device for improving the quality or quantity of work performed. As they attempt to superimpose the techniques on their basically negative view of people, they miss the essence, and the program fails.

There is a history of using the behavioral sciences to develop new tools for improving worker output. After World War II, management turned its attention to the people factors of production and tried to apply scientific techniques there, too. Applications of science to the management of people have generally treated people as response mechanisms. Little has been done to study and respond to people's inner motivations. In fact, managers often speak of "motivating" workers, ignoring the evidence that motivation comes from within the individual — that the task of management is to present the factors to which the worker's motivations will respond.

Not all managers are concerned with the people factors in production. "There is great resistance in top management circles, once you get beyond lip service, to the idea that human resources are a key to improving productivity and competitive effectiveness," says Daniel Yankelovich. They think that capital investment, technology, and management systems are more important. Mr. Yankelovich's explanation for this is that "many of the people in top management are trained in finance or engineering or production. They are not as comfortable with the intangibles of human behavior as with the more tangible areas of business. Also, in the past, technology and capital investment *were* the key factors — and were, in addition, easier to deal with."

Managers, understandably, stayed with what they knew best. But today they are being forced to consider the people aspects of managing as the old concepts of work and organization fail to produce satisfactory results. The systems to which people refuse to conform will have to be adapted to the irrationalities, emotions, feelings, needs, and wants of the managed and the managers.

As part of the social upheaval of the postwar era, managers have been less isolated from non-managers than their predecessors were. They not only find it quite natural to relate with workers, they see their own fate tied closely to that of the people they manage.

"The essence of good management is the art of knowing, understanding, and fulfilling human needs," says one corporate vice president. "For if only the manager is getting his needs fulfilled at the expense of his people, and they are getting little if any satisfaction, it's only win for him and lose for them. This is not only unhealthy, it's stupid, for people won't put up with a losing situation for very long."

In this age of unleashed human demands, even the most hard-nosed managers cannot fail to see that they are managing *people* and that they themselves are people with more dimensions than the managerial role formerly called for. The effective manager has to be more than a practitioner of the technologies available. Techniques for financial analysis, decision-making, business forecasting, information systems operation, and even interpreting human behavior cannot compensate for the lack of heart in a manager.

A computer can make a decision for you. But as a manager, you have to provide the heart to execute that decision. You must make the value judgments to ensure that what may be right economically and technically is also "right" with people — that what is about to be done will fit the moral and ethical climate. You must sense and solve the many human problems involved in carrying out that decision. And you have to have the guts to live with your decision.

Managers who are high achievers are as concerned about people as they are about production, according to Teleometrics International after a study of 16,000 managers in 50 organizations. Analyzing the managers themselves and the perceptions of their subordinates in this five-year project, Teleometrics concluded that high achievers differed from other managers in their search for personal satisfaction in the job and in their effort to provide the opportunity for their subordinates to do so. They actively communicate — sending and receiving — with their associates, and they involve their subordinates in decision-making.

HUMANAGEMENT: THE ULTIMATE STYLE

The pressure for humanistic management applies to more than managerial relationships with employees. Giving the worker what he or she wants depends partly on how the manager perceives the company relating to society in terms of product, social concern and involvement, and environmental impact. The manager's effectiveness is influenced by the whole context in which the company operates. It is determined, too, by the manager's self concept. A manager must understand how his actions affect workers, shareholders, customers, and the public.

The character of management in the years ahead might better be described by the term "humanagement." That would remind us what it is that is managed, for whom, by whom, and in what manner. Humanagement will represent change across the entire scope of the manager's role. The successful corporation of the future will:

- Deal with all aspects of the business in ways that reflect appreciation for people as whole persons.

- Find ways to enable the worker to invest more talent into the job and derive meaning and personal growth from it.

- Appreciate the human relationships within an organization and between the organization and the outside world.

- Take an optimistic view of people, building on cooperation rather than on conflict.

- Permit the manager to reveal himself as a human being with with fears, wants, and the need for growth.

Humanagement may sound like a soft style of managing — or not managing at all. This could not be further from the truth. Responding to people is far more difficult than following rules that treat them as simple response mechanisms. Acting as a complete person, and regarding others as such, is far more demanding than settling for distant relationships with two-dimensional figures.

With the addition of the people factor, the managerial function increases exponentially. Managers will have to master the very factors they have been taught to ignore. Many are already aware that the emotional content of their relations with others is critical to their performance. They can see that screening out human values — their own and others' — raises the odds for making a bad decision. Humanistic as managers may have wanted to be, they had been taught to leave that part of themselves outside the plant or office. Now, that quality is becoming central to the managerial role. Organizations built on depersonalizing relations will now have to humanize them.

Management was neat and simple when people were not a factor with which to be concerned, or when they were merely something to be manipulated. But the equation for good management is changing. Managers who have been *efficient* under the old standards have to undergo new tests for *effectiveness* in determining what the new standards are and in dealing with them.

Rather than mastering people and resisting change, the manager must now master change and resolve people's many needs. This does not mean yielding to every request or pressure; it requires awareness and involvement in order to determine which issues to respond to and which to oppose. As the old concepts of hierarchy and domination crumble, managerial authority comes not from the manager's position so much as from his or her knowledge of, and effectiveness in, dealing with people.

The managers of the future will see beyond these difficulties that surround their role. They will find increased opportunity to express themselves at work and to derive more satisfaction from it. They will bring the technology of their jobs together with their own humanism, welcoming the opportunity to play broader roles — for they too have been the victims of Taylorism. Beneath the trappings of office, there have always been people with wants, needs, fears, weaknesses, and aspirations. Now they can admit that they are human. In fact, they had better reveal their humanity if they want to succeed.

The ascent of humanagement does not signal the end of scientific management. That would entail an unlikely and undesirable loss of valuable tools for accomplishing work. Today's effective managers are already pointing the way to combining scientific technique with humanistic behavior.

It is now possible — and necessary — for a manager to be both efficient and human at the same time, says Dr. Frederick Herzberg, distinguished professor of management, University of Utah, and the father of job enrichment. Dr. Herzberg, who is also a contributing editor to *Industry Week,* writes: "We must reverse the fragmentation process inherent in our post-industrial society and strive to bring a wholeness back to the individual."

Humanagement will be the mastery of organizations built of whole people, serving whole people.

2
The Manager of the Future

A manager works with information and people. In the years ahead, the typical manager will have more control over information and less control over people.

The words "control" and "manager" may take on new meanings. In the opinion of many executives and students of management, the manager's role will become that of a negotiator — coordinating the capabilities, wants, and needs of the many forces surrounding that position.

The manager will work in a climate shaped by new conditions:

- Our economy will be growing at a much slower rate in the latter years of this century than it has in the past quarter-century. Most economists and futurists see real gains running at about half the rate of years in which today's managers learned their trade. That means there will be less room for error and there will be new yardsticks for success.

- The trend toward bigness in corporations will not be reversed. Government involvement in business activities encourages growth by merger rather than by innovation and favors corporations large enough to deal with the regulatory burden. Despite Americans' aversion to large corporations, giants will be needed to compete against the big overseas firms and to muster the resources and technology needed to meet our social challenges.

- The cost of such things as pollution control, health, and safety will be folded into the corporate cost structure and everyone will pay the price. Sensitivity to many of society's wants will have a dollars-and-cents value.

- An age of conservation will drastically change what we manufacture and how we do it.

- The regulatory rub against corporate freedom will be at least as comprehensive as it is today; the best management can hope for is a cooperative spirit between industry and government and an atmosphere in which performance guidelines are negotiated rather than decreed.

What a company can do will not be determined by its internal capabilities alone. Increasingly, it will be bound by externally imposed restraints. Society's expectations have been raised, and, although the specific demands may vary from time to time, the momentum is too great to be reversed.

In this diverse society, people are joining together in groups for special purposes. As any or all of them levy their requests on the corporation, the chief executive will have to balance these conflicting interests. Top management is, therefore, being forced to take the lead in interchange and negotiation.

Cracks have already developed in the ownership of our major corporations, allowing varied interests to express themselves inside the company. We have already seen stockholders seeking objectives other than profit. In late 1978, for example, a group of nuns, holding 4000 shares of Lykes Corporation stock, introduced a resolution at the company's annual meeting, calling for the company to hold open certain steelmaking facilities in Youngstown. Their motive: to preserve jobs in the area. "The day has passed when a giant corporation can with impunity close a plant, put thousands out of work, and devastate a community as though those workers and that community had no interest or stake in the company's decision," said one of the sisters.

Understandably, then, a major portion of top management's time, especially in the larger corporations, is devoted to determining what these interest groups are and what their demands will be. As they sort their way through this maze of conflict and contradiction, management is making the corporation relevant to the society in which it exists.

Today, management is in a pressure cooker, answering to any and all challengers as well as to those stockholders who are concerned about financial return. In the future, however, as the interest groups acquire an increasing share of American business, management may find itself in the role of a negotiator or consultant, laying out the alternatives, explaining the tradeoffs, and letting the owners them-selves resolve the conflict.

Some of these same forces are bubbling within the corporation itself. The quest for identity, self-actualization, material comforts, and a "say" in what business does come from the lowest levels of the workforce and the middle ranks of management. On this front, too, management is forced to play negotiator rather than controller.

Because they will be dealing with divisive issues, managers will rely more on their personal values and their ability to appreciate the values of others. This is why some top executives say the job will demand a person who is more intellectual and reflective than in the past, and one who is brave enough to address the issues head on.

RENAISSANCE MAN RETURNS

Aloof, all-powerful, free to deploy resources and people as he chooses. If that image of the corporate chief executive officer still fits any industry leaders, it may soon fade. Contrary to what the public may think, chief executives are not primarily concerned with finances or products and services. They perceive themselves as for-ward observers of the climate in which their companies operate and as the conductors of an orchestra of workers. They have found that the higher they climb in management, the less freedom they have — and the greater the number of forces bearing on them.

In the large corporations, the person at the top has to assess the company's interaction with federal, state, and local governments here and abroad, and with other groups outside the company. Op-erating as a corporate statesman, this person works with a "cabi-net" of advisers and experts to determine how a proposed course of action will affect all facets of the business and all the outside groups with which the company interfaces.

Like the Renaissance Man, the future executive will have a broad intellectual reach. Renaissance Man was total. He was not defined in terms of any single discipline. He tried his hand at everything and lived in an idea-rich atmosphere. His was an age that saw the beginnings of modern physical science. It was a time for questioning, a time for challenging the old order.

Because of the need to bring the best ideas together from many disciplines and management functions, management experts foresee the widespread acceptance of a more collaborative style of leadership up and down the corporate ladder. The determinant of a manager's success may well be his ability to attract and work with experts who operate as his cabinet, sensitizing him to all the problems that should be considered and helping him arrive at sound decisions. By contrast, the authoritarian manager asserts his will, demanding conformance rather than drawing upon the initiative and talents of others. That style will not provide strong enough management for the organizations of the future! Although there may not be enough Renaissance men and women to head each organization, the doors are open for the manager who is sufficiently multi-disciplined and able to surround himself with talented people to create a "Renaissance team."

THE DEMISE OF THE AUTOCRAT

Confidence in the effectiveness of one-man rule has been shattered in an increasingly democratic society and shamed by the greater strength found in collaboration. Business has become too complex and fast-moving to permit a company to tie its fortunes to one mind and depend on one person to anticipate and evaluate every potential problem and opportunity. In smaller companies, one person can reasonably successfully shoulder all the duties, but even this person needs the support of a strong corps of talented assistants.

Most companies are headed by one person. The buck has to stop somewhere, as they say. Few of these people *rule,* however. You would have a hard time finding a top executive who doesn't insist that he or she has to rely on others for information, if not for guidance. Some see it the other way around, in fact. They see their role as that of a guiding influence; they watch carefully that their suggestions are not construed as orders that would inhibit independent thinking by their subordinates.

Semon (Bunky) Knudsen — with a reputation for tough, domineering management first at Ford, General Motors, and then White Motor Corporation — admits: "There have been darn few times when I've made a hard, cold decision without advice from my staff. And at least a couple of those were very painful. They've been seared in my memory, to say the least!"

The autocratic ruler has the advantage of being able to move fast, to make decisions quickly, and push for instant implementation, bulldozing the way over differences of opinion. Unfortunately, this ruler's opinion is not always the right one. Right or wrong, differences of opinion fester among subordinates and hamper the implementation of the boss's decision. There is less and less room for error in business and more and more reason to ensure that employees understand, and feel part of, the action. The dictator's territory is shrinking fast.

The upper echelons of management have held no monopoly on one-man rule. A division chief, department head, or plant manager may run a given territory with an iron hand, regardless of the atmosphere in the rest of the company. In the years ahead, it is possible that companies will bring in highly mobile top executives with special talents to meet their special circumstances at various times. This turnover at the top — a sort of blood transfusion — would depend on strong lower echelons to provide stability and continuity. Dictatorial middle managers might, therefore, encounter even less opposition from above than they do now. On the other hand, in those large companies that decentralize their operating units and allow managers down the line to operate as entrepreneurs, the need for creativity and high performance could force these managers to draw upon all the expertise they can find.

Today, outside pressures work against one person's ruling at the top. A significant change in the role of the board of directors and in the officerships will occur either through legislation and regulation or through voluntary adaptation. There are cases of inside directors yielding to the chairman, since they are the employees and he is the boss. Outside directors likewise can be puppets who hold their position through friendship with the chairman or through a client relationship (lawyers and accountants). Future boards of directors will be held more responsible for actions of the corporation. In theory, a president is hired to run the company, and the board of directors hires and oversees the president on general policy and direction. In recent years, however, companies of all sizes have permitted the chairman of the board to serve also as the chief executive. Whether or not this person bears the second title – president – he is, in effect, both employer and employee! This doesn't necessarily establish one-man rule, but it invites it if the board of directors does not challenge, or evaluate the performance of, its own chairman – the hired professional.

Some companies have separated executive from operating duties. One set of duties involves corporate strategy – studying the economic-social-political climate and positioning the resources of the company for the most effective response to change or anticipated change. The other involves operating those businesses. These sets of duties require different kinds of people, with different talents and orientations. The person who tries to wear both hats runs the risk of being an expert at one and an amateur at the other.

By themselves, the traditional titles "chairman" and "president" no longer describe for sure what a person does. For that reason, key responsibilities are designated differently in some companies by assigning the titles "chief executive officer," "chief operating officer," and "chief financial officer."

Whatever his or her title – and accountability to the board – the person at the top is becoming so involved with external relations and long-range strategy that some internal duties must be delegated. Therefore, the manager can no longer call all the shots. This does not mean that the chief executive can abdicate any ultimate responsibilities, but that they can be *delegated,* with the manager stepping in as a referee to resolve differences of opinion when they occur. At all levels, the more effective managers are spreading the load and capitalizing on the potential within their people. They are promoting such concepts as participative mangement and job enrichment down the line.

FREED BY THE COMPUTER TO MANAGE

Top managers see people relationships as the area of growing importance for themselves and for managers down the line. Business-technical-operational information can be obtained and managed relatively easily compared to sorting out people's wants, needs, talents, experience, and responsibilities.

Although we are undergoing an information revolution, this will not diminish the manager's role. It will change it and enlarge it. The manager will have to know what goes in and what can come out of the information system, but this will be a tool — neither the manager's master nor replacement. The information systems that will best serve management will be streamlined and made responsive to people. There will be no blinking monster running the entire show, spewing mountains of useless paper out on intimidated humans. Management experts see, instead, a greatly decentralized information system responding to inquiries rather than merely emitting periodic reports.

After its early fascination with the computer, management now realizes that not all business decisions can be made with a calculator or computer. Relying on mathematics tends to simplify a problem, and there is the danger that you will begin dealing with something that bears little resemblance to the real problem.

The managers of the future will receive much of their data via electronic display — either on portable minicomputers or on conveniently located terminals (or portable ones) which connect with a central computer. They will have at their fingertips information on their machines, their money, their units' performance up-to-the-minute, corporate performance, and worldwide economic data, as well as libraries of technical and legal information. They will be able to test alternative actions before giving instructions to their people. They will be better able to anticipate the impact of their actions on other operations of the company, and vice versa.

This accessibility of information is going to give the manager more freedom — freedom to be a manager more of the time. For the middle manager, who probably worries most about the impact of the computer, it will mean release from mundane calculations and access to information which either was not available before or which was not available on a current basis. Improved information means that the manager can do a better job of managing. But there is a catch in this benefit. Because the manager can do a better job of managing, he or she will be expected to do a better job. This new-found freedom will not be a blank check. The manager will be working toward agreed objectives and will be judged against higher standards of performance. Fortunately, it will be possible to make better decisions, thanks to the constant feedback from the information system. Because the technical and operating data available will be improved, the manager will be able to devote more time to the people aspects of managing. The middle manager will have the opportunity to be more of a real manager than ever before.

The ability to call up data from an infinite number of work locations will support the current trend toward decentralization and the dispersal of decision-making. The first use of data processing systems resulted in centralization, particularly in accounting. In the future, however, it will permit a decentralization of operational decision-making, giving workers the capability to manage themselves to a greater degree. The distinct line between manager and worker could grow fuzzy. In some situations, we may see managerless work groups, in which workers would be entrusted with routine decisions. They would consult with a professional or resource person rather than being managed by a conventional "boss."

NEW FACES IN THE RANKS

Restructuring management work will proceed as quickly as the supply of managers suited for it permits. This will require a new breed of manager — a breed in terms of attitude, not age group. While many managers resist change in the nature of their work, some of today's managers have been the changers. Managers in their forties and fifties have taken the first steps toward humanagement, as well as developing the technologies that open the way for it.

Most of the hands at the helm of today's industrial organizations are wrinkled with experience and raw-knuckled from hard knocks. A few, however, are only blistered by a rapid climb up the corporate ladder. The growing number of young chief executive officers is proof that the doors have been opened to a broader age span, suggesting that competence and adaptability are replacing seniority as the prime requirements for the top spot.

But the custom of "paying your dues" hasn't faded away. A would-be top manager still has to prove himself, but it can be done in fewer years. Seniority is no guarantee of ability. The manager who relies too heavily on it will lose out to the young, aggressive manager who proves his or her competence and demonstrates potential for carrying the load. Seniority does not accurately reflect experience, either. A manager with the vigor and stamina of youth can compress a lot of experience into relatively few years, crossing functional lines and changing companies, and becoming exposed to more learning and testing than a manager who spends 30 or 40 years working up the more conventional routes.

Conventional routes are still the convention, however. The man or woman who rises to the top in relatively few years is bucking tradition. But this tradition may not have much of a future. It's not a very old tradition anyway. As one 39-year-old president and chairman points out: "In the early days of this country there were a lot of young people who signed the Declaration of Independence; a lot of young people managed companies."

As industries matured — railroads, shipping, mining, and metals production, for instance — they formulated elaborate customs and practices. A key part of the management role was the protection of the organization from undue change; attainment of top management positions depended on mastering the history of the industry and the company. More recently, however, the emergence of new industries has helped propel some young managers to the top. Young industries such as electronics don't have people around with 30 years' experience. Fast-growing, high-technology companies; the conglomerates; and some of the new service industries require the latest in technological and managerial know-how. That's not always found in managers who are long on seniority.

SPECIAL PROBLEMS FOR YOUNG MANAGERS

Despite fast movement and broad experience, the young executive is likely to admit, when pressed, that he or she was initially overwhelmed with the magnitude of the job upon assuming the top office. Realization that your decision determines where your company is going can hit hard. No matter how much you rationally consider the weight of responsibility, you can't fully appreciate it until it falls on you.

One young chief executive recalls the shock of realizing that "the buck not only stops here; it also starts here." Others say they were ready and able to respond quickly and effectively to all the problems that bombarded them except one — the time required to implement action through others. Balancing people's opinions, developing new policies, and initiating change can be a slow process.

One thing that can get in the way of speedy decision-making and action is the resentment of the young executive by those who have been passed over. Involving these people meaningfully in the decision-making process may help overcome this resentment, but some subordinates may drag their heels anyway. That is why companies try to designate a new chief executive well in advance of his or her appointment and make sure that this individual's accomplishments and strengths are well publicized. They hope that the selection will be above reproach for the most part, and they want time to work on those few persons who are apt to be unreasonably resentful.

The young person at the top sometimes encounters older subordinates anxious to serve as teachers. This can be good or bad. They can offer valuable guidance and direction. On the other hand, they may be anxious to greet every new idea with an example of how that one was tried before and failed. This beard-stroking will neutralize the young executive who hasn't done enough homework to anticipate some of the questions and solutions offered by these elders.

The apparent increase in the number of top executives in their late thirties and early forties seems to suggest that managers of the future will be younger and younger. But this is not necessarily so. The manager who was 40 years old in 1975 was born in 1935 — a year with one of the lowest birthrates in recent history. It wasn't being part of a large peer group that propelled this person into top management. If there has been a shift toward younger executives, it has been for reasons such as better education, broader experience, and better performance.

An *Industry Week* survey of managers of all ages shows that they regard the manager in his or her forties as the most effective. At this age, a manager has acquired experience while retaining some of the drive of youth. People are generally more willing to work for someone in this age range, the managers say. The "young whippersnapper" may not have enough years of experience to win confident followers. And the manager nearing retirement is too set in the old ways — too interested in relying on experience and too unwilling to try new ideas. The manager between 40 and 50 is regarded as most likely to be broadminded; this person doesn't expect to have a monopoly on good ideas and knows that "there is more than one way to skin a cat."

There has been no need, so far as sheer numbers are concerned, to dip into the younger age brackets for an increasing share of top executives. The manager just turned 40 who heads a corporation is not in that position because of a shortage of older candidates. During the 1970's, there were more Americans in the 45 to 65 bracket than in the 30 to 45 range.

People born in the post-World War II baby boom are now entering their thirties. Some are already in management, armed with degrees and the latest management technology. Their ripening into senior management age bodes both good and bad for the corporation. There will be more candidates for key positions. These young managers may be a little hungrier to learn, perform, and even conform, but those who crowd for promotion and fail will pose a serious challenge to management in their demands for meaningful, rewarding work.

During the 1980's, these people could tend to lower the average age in management. But they will pull the average upward in the 1990's and beyond. The next wave of newcomers, arriving in the 1990's, may find themselves latecomers blocked by the old, baby boom managers who have settled into their late forties and fifties, entrenched in management positions. In the latter part of this century, then, management ranks could be swollen with older — not younger — people than today.

The recent raising of the mandatory retirement age to 70 from 65 could intensify this squeeze on the available management spots. Management will have to do some delicate management of its own ranks in order to avoid frustrating people trying to move up in responsibility. In heated competition for the opportunity to manage, many old biases — age, sex, and race — will have to be set aside in favor of demonstrated competence as the critereon for promotion.

Each year, more and more women and members of minority races and ethnic groups will enter the management ranks, and there is no reason to doubt that some will reach top positions. In recent years, equal employment legislation has opened the doors for the non-traditional managerial candidate. Some managers fear that over-correction of previous inequities is putting unqualified people on fast tracks for promotion and that this will dilute the effectiveness of management. On the other hand, nepotism, the selection of managers on the basis of old friendships or school ties, and other practices of the past have not always produced first-rate managers.

"YOUNG" VALUES

At ease with the computer, closed-circuit television, and rapid change, the young manager has assets which his or her company needs and which its senior executives may not have. Today's younger managers are more effective than young managers of past generations and are capable of effecting more change in their companies than their predecessors, say the managers responding to the *Industry Week* survey. The under-40 manager is far better prepared than before, thanks to the improved educational foundation available. Some credit, too, has to go to employers for providing training and educational support. Because of this improved preparation, an individual can be entrusted with greater responsibility after fewer years' experience than in the past. The group still sees a gap between the young and the more experienced managers, however. Managers of all ages rank the 40- to 50-year-olds as better equipped and more effective.

Comparisons of the young and the old reveal some differences in attitudes and values that could have important implications for the future. In the *Industry Week* study, for example, the scales tipped in favor of the young manager when it comes to awareness of people and their motivations. The younger manager is more inclined to reject the military approach to managing. On the other hand, it should be recognized that much of the openness and change that has swept through our organizations in the last decade or two has to be credited largely to upper and middle level managers who have staged a quiet but significant revolution. The "younger" attitudes prevailing in organizations today are due to those whose chronological youth is some distance behind them.

The difference between "young" and "old" isn't always a factor of age, and what appears to be a real difference is sometimes only a communications problem. The older manager's jargon may be a little dated, but that doesn't mean he or she hasn't kept current. In fact, some of the young manager's business school jargon may simply be words that are part of an attempt to describe things the senior manager "automatically" does well.

Some differences between younger and older managers can be expected because of the experiences the two have had during comparable periods in their lives. They may have entered industry at quite different entry points with far different responsibilities, recognition, and compensation. One old tiger points out: "We haven't had their perspective, which is almost thirty years of unrestricted economic growth, improving life-styles, the new environmental ethic, and social reform ethic. It would be wrong to expect them not to be different."

The younger manager is sometimes a paradox both to himself and to his superiors. Despite an outspoken concern for others and for social issues, he is apt to be self-oriented to a high degree. The young manager's schooling sometimes has led him to be a lone competitor who may have much to learn about operating as a team member.

The under-40 manager often gives the impression of being less profit-oriented than older managers. Yet 85 percent of these younger executives recognize that they *should be* as profit-oriented as older managers. The discrepancy may be due to definition or perspective. Many tend to see profit as "not the only priority" of business. As a 32-year-old puts it: "To keep going, you have to make a profit." But, she quickly adds, "now there is a serious commitment to try to make industry more relevant to the people who are working in it."

The seeming lack of profit-orientation may also be linked to the way many young managers view their work and their careers. Their interests are divided. Having learned that life is more than work, they often jealously guard their personal time; they are not 100 percent dedicated to the company 100 percent of the time. Yet they are credited with working hard when they do work. It's possible that their off-hours activities make them even more effective managers. If they mix work with other interests they enjoy, possibly even learn something applicable to the job, or simply relax and return to work refreshed, they help themselves and the organization. The nose-to-the-grindstone, profits-above-all-else approach to business is dying (if it is not already dead). There is no reason to expect young managers to be any different from some of their elders who take a more "modern" view of work. There is a gap between those of the old philosophy and the new, but it is not based on age differences.

The inquisitiveness of young managers may further feed notions that they are not really interested in profits, hard work, or company loyalty. Youth has always been inquisitive, and, in today's business world, there is more opportunity to exercise this than ever before. Young managers freely challenge others as to why things are being done or how they are done. They ask questions outside their areas of responsibility. They stretch to see the bigger picture. This may be good for the health of the organization or it may add up to nothing more than question-and-answer games. Whether inquisitiveness is genuine and will work toward developing better managers depends on the individual. Sometimes young managers are accused of worrying too much about the generalities and being impatient with details — concerning themselves with corporate strategy and neglecting the day-to-day tactics for which they are responsible. Those who have business degrees, in particular, have been taught to look at the big picture — at corporate strategy as opposed to mundane, everyday departmental tasks. This can render them impatient with anything less than sweeping problems. Senior management is, therefore, challenged to help younger managers focus on the current details without destroying their broader capability.

If young managers are bringing with them greater awareness of people and a broader view of profit and work, they will accelerate the trend to humanagement started by their predecessors. Their personal needs and their resistance to hierarchy will exert leverage for major institutional change. Their very presence in the management ranks — breaking traditional barriers on age, sex, and race — already demonstrate the impact of new values on the corporation.

WOMEN IN A "MAN'S WORLD"

Doors to the management ranks are open wide for young people with talent. They are beginning to creak open slowly for members of racial or ethnic minorities. But values, practices, and customs are being shattered by the rush of women into middle management. The traditional expectations of what a woman should be are giving way to seeing young women managers as managers first and women second. Despite the fact that all the questions of protocol haven't been worked out, the number of women managers will grow fast in the next two decades. By the year 2000, more than half the workforce will be women. Their impact on management will be profound.

Some women have shown that they can be feminine, yet effective as managers. Many of the men, meanwhile, are trying to understand just what this means in terms of day-to-day behavior. It's not acceptable for a woman manager to resort to tears to get her own way, most managers agree, but it may be all right to hold the door open for her — it *may* be, that is, and then again it may not. Most men don't mind opening doors for a woman, but they are learning to determine, on a case-by-case basis, whether the woman minds.

Most men have been taught to see themselves as strong, rational, objective, and controlled. Women have been taught to see them that way, too. Both have, until recently, been taught to regard women as emotional, irrational, seductive, sensitive, and weak. The stereotypes of both men and women are being challenged. But, until they have been discarded, they will work against women in management and against the organization's likelihood of selecting from all the best managerial candidates. Stereotyping has led men to feel that they have to be supportive of women — not compete against them. While today's women are ready to compete, not all men can reciprocate. They can try, but not always without mixed emotions.

Custom and culture rendered women "unsuited" for management for centuries — for most of history, for that matter. But they just might be naturals for management work. Several years ago, the Johnson O'Connor Research Foundation, Inc. of New York identified 22 basic management aptitudes and found no sexual differences in 14 of them. Of the remaining eight, women excel in six!

Aptitudes in which the foundation says there are no discernible sex differences include analytical reasoning, eyedness (a measure of left-right cerebral dominance), foresight, inductive reasoning, memory for design, number memory, objective personality, subjective personality, pitch discrimination, rhythm memory (which includes physical coordination), timbre discrimination, tonal memory, general knowledge (as measured by vocabulary tests), and tweezer dexterity.

Men excell in grip — not unimportant when it comes to handshaking and toting briefcases and luggage. They outdo women in structural visualization — a trait central to technical and scientific professions.

Women are "naturals" when it comes to accounting aptitude, "ideaphoria" (the rate of flow of ideas used in activities involving persuasion and verbal fluency), verbalizing, observation of small changes, finger dexterity, and abstract visualization.

Women hold about 1 out of 20 of today's management positions. Although they are no longer a rarity, they still command extra attention, and they are still fighting to get to the top of large companies. Those who hold vice presidential spots are primarily in staff positions; women have not yet gained much access to line management with bottom-line responsibility.

The absence of women in upper management is a relatively new problem because women managers have become serious contenders only in the last 10 or 15 years. Seasoned women managers can see that the demands for the higher positions call for more experience than women have generally been able to acquire. They realize, too, that not all men make it to those few top positions. The loudest complaints about the unfairness of the game, therefore, do not come from women in management. They admit they haven't been there long enough to reach the top, and many of them did not begin their careers with that in mind. Until recently, a woman went to work just to have a job. If she did eventually find herself in a career, she did not expect to advance far.

Women have higher expectations today. With more of them in the "pipeline," some of the practices which barred their progress are under intense pressure to fold. And with more of them around, the chance that some will reach the top is improving on the basis of sheer numbers.

Few women managers are activists in the women's movement. They generally want to be seen as professional — not radical. They realize that hostility will not help them in the ways that will contribute most to their acceptance and advancement. One of the biggest handicaps women have is the lack of access to the informal management structure, the opportunity to engage in the after-hours or golf course chatter, and the chance to be groomed by a mentor. Carrying their womanhood like a cross will only heighten this barrier.

It will take time to erode the customs that still make management a man's world. Business language, for example, bears a lot of the military or sports flavor — "game plan," "battle plan," "heavy artillery," "troops" — terms with which men are more comfortable than women. Even when they are being helpful, male managers sometimes inadvertently let the woman manager know that she is entering a man's world.

Treating the female vice president like a secretary is a slip-up that will disappear in time as people begin to realize that not all women are secretaries or clerks. As women managers demonstrate their effectiveness to more and more workers, resentment over working for a woman boss will ease. Resentment is not likely to disappear totally, however; it never has for male bosses. Some women managers have been able to settle comfortably into their jobs because they realize that many of their problems are the problems of managers rather than attacks on women.

A minority of male managers hold the "over my dead body" attitude toward female peers. In general, women find the younger men easier to work with. They're more likely to have been exposed to the new school of thought, they've worked with women as peers in school, and their wives may be pursuing careers. Their receptiveness will work toward accelerating the number of women in management in the years ahead.

ROUTES TO THE TOP

The best paths for advancement for young men and women will become even less clear than in the past. Companies headed by a person who came up the ranks in production used to tend to select a production man to fill the spot on his retirement. Companies headed by a marketing man would pick another marketing man. And so it went. Today, a company may make a deliberate change in the type of person at the top to meet particular needs at a particular time. Since there aren't many Renaissance men or women around, a chief executive is sometimes brought in to head a company for two or three years in order to lend a specific expertise to solving priority problems. Even these "generalists" often have a strong suit of functional expertise.

As always, there will be no single path to the top. But there may be some shifts in the functional areas that provide the best preparation. A financial background promises to be the most popular route to the top in the years immediately ahead, since one of the prime responsibilities of top management is the structuring and controlling of companies. A good understanding of the sources and management of capital will be crucial in the decade ahead. Losing ground since the booming 1960's, when the corporate objective was to meet every whim of the consumer, the marketing manager still has fairly good odds of making it to the top — particularly if he or she is a strategist rather than an over-titled sales manager.

The person with an engineering background is gaining popularity for the top spot, since technology assessment is increasingly important in determining corporate strategy; management has to appreciate the technological alternatives in terms of the product, production processes, and regulatory impact. This manager seems to be gaining ground at the expense of the production-oriented person who may be more limited in scope and less future-oriented.

The internationalization of business will change the nature of many functional specialities. For example, as U.S. manufacturers build production facilities overseas, the manufacturing manager will no longer be simply the person who runs the plant. The job will entail dealing with international supplies of materials, tariffs, local laws, and cultural differences among workers. To reach the top, a manager — particularly in the larger companies — will have to be more world-cognizant. He or she will have to understand management practices, local customs, business conditions, and worker attitudes in numerous countries.

The future executive will have to think more strategically whether he or she is heading up a particular functional area in the organization or the total organization. It will not be sufficient to react to conditions or play hunches. Where it was once enough to "know the business," the future executive will have to understand the total business environment.

Whatever functional area a person is in, there will be little chance for upward movement without the ability to relate to other functional areas in the company. The mark of a good manager will be the knack of working cooperatively with experts in a variety of "unrelated" fields. Building on a solid base of know-how in one functional area, a manager will have to develop into a generalist as well. To get to the top, the new manager will have to be broad-gauged and multi-disciplined. On that, few chief executives or management experts disagree. That clearly indicates that the manager of the future will be a learner — a person whose education never ceases.

3
Professionals Without a Profession

Staffing the corporation with strong management has never been an easy task. The expertise and talents needed from one management position to another vary widely. Because of the traditional hierarchical structure of organizations, the talents and skills required at the bottom are dramatically different from those needed at the top. Those at the bottom strain to master a functional specialty; managers at the top have to be generalists; those in the middle struggle to make the transition. Because of the explosion of knowledge in the growing number of areas with which management is concerned, the individual faces an increasingly difficult task of preparation.

Because management is not a clearly defined profession, neither the corporation nor the managerial candidates have known exactly what to look for or to prepare for. Using the best scientific and human relations tools, business executives have pursued their work as a profession. They have acquired skills which are universal enough to enable them to move from company to company and from industry to industry. Their performance has been judged against some fairly universally accepted standards.

Management has yet to become a profession, however. It requires no licensing or certification, although it offers good status and financial rewards. It encompasses many skills which are transferable, but presents no solid body of knowledge. It is based not on a unified discipline but upon borrowings from many fields.

What passes for rules and truths are simply the practices that have worked in the past. Nearly all the management schools were born after World War II. Much of the content of their curriculum is a distillation or approximation of the techniques developed by great managers, who practiced their craft before the schools were established, or by today's successful managers, who offer their own new twists to managing organizations. Properly used, these techniques help the good manager emulate the excellent manager.

Management seems to be growing closer to a profession, but since it involves art as well as science, and feelings as well as facts, it may never become one. Nevertheless, managers are "professional" in their approach to the role they play. For the time being, and maybe always, they will operate as professionals without a profession. Perhaps a profession would be too limiting — running counter to the concept of Renaissance people — since virtually all bodies of knowledge may be relevant to managing.

As society forces business to reexamine and broaden its role, managers will find their scope of responsibility expanding ever wider. In terms of education, background, and viewpoints, they often feel a kinship to their counterparts in government and academia. The job is changing in real terms and in the way newcomers to the "profession" see it. It will be shaped by thousands of individuals as they respond to new demands and opportunities.

THROW AWAY THE IDEAL MOLD

Top managers, almost without exception, insist that management development is up to the individual. Although companies often provide management development programs, they see this as furnishing only the setting in which the individual can make a manager of himself. Until a few years ago, development programs were select clubs; if a person showed promise, he or she was "put into" a management development program. Recently, companies have been scrapping the notion that there is an ideal mold for managers. Guided by the humanistic assumption that management potential is broadly dispersed, they offer training programs in the university or cafeteria approach. Rather than designing a formal curriculum for a select few, they make a variety of courses,

seminars, and other learning experiences available to virtually anyone who wants them.

Although companies do some singling out of promising managerial candidates, the emphasis has swung to letting people gravitate
toward the possibility of success, with the idea that managerial
talent will emerge if the company provides the opportunities.

"People have tended to put managers through a program because
it was the fad," recalls the head of a large management development center. "No diagnosis was made of what the individual manager needed." In the last few years, companies have backed off
somewhat in formal programs of study and job progression as they
have come to appreciate individuals' different needs.

A company may choose either to leave the selection of development courses entirely up to the individuals, or to counsel them in
planning their development paths. Most people can benefit from
counseling. Not everyone has the necessary self-awareness to know
what strengths can be built upon and what weak areas need strengthening. Many lack the discipline to overcome the tendency to stick
to what they like or already know.

"WHAT'S GOING ON AROUND HERE?"

The problems of management are no longer just technical or just
financial. Today an engineer or a salesman arrives in a management
position and is suddenly buffeted with all sorts of problems for
which he has acquired no tools, no experience, and no guidance.
A manager has to learn while managing; as new things come up,
they must be synthesized. The fundamental requirement for development, therefore, is the ability to learn. What and how a
manager learns determines whether he or she is suited for the jobs
that come along. The first thing that some top executives look for
in managerial candidates is that positive force called "initiative."
Others call it "eagerness" — a person's willingness to dig in and
work hard at developing new skills, broadening the job, and even
taking the risk of doing the job so well that it is eliminated. It
takes courage and resilience to shape yourself into a manager and
to bounce back when you fail at some aspect of the challenge. As
one company president puts it: "You don't win every day. You

don't always accomplish your objectives. The good manager is the guy who can come back from defeat."

Few managers find themselves in a position where they have all the information they need to perform well — much less to develop their potential for a more demanding job. The farther they are from the top, the less they know about the big picture. The higher they rise from the bottom rungs of the corporate ladder, the less they can keep up with the details.

There are signs that read: "If you aren't thoroughly confused, you don't know what's going on around here." Some managers may be uninformed and not care about it, or they may know enough to get through the day but not enough to cut through the confusion. Some managers make decisions on very little information. They aren't enlightened or involved enough to play hunches well. The effective manager is highly sensitive to what he does not know and constantly battles to eliminate confusion. "A good manager, to truly contribute, must know what is going on all the time," says one corporate president. "Knowledge is power. He must insist that communication flows upward and downward. What makes the really successful manager exceptional is that he is continually and successfully seeking better ways to function. He questions the *status quo,* and he analyzes his areas of responsibility with a facts-oriented objective viewpoint, being ready to discard what has been done over the years if the new way is apparently a better way."

To be effective calls for being informed about:

- Company goals.
- Your own goals and key duties.
- Your employees' key duties and capabilities.
- Other department's goals and capabilities.
- Policies and procedures you'll have to live with or change.
- The limits of your "authority" — what you can do on your own, what needs to be reported, what needs prior approval.

Even in the most enlightened, progressive companies, people don't have all this information handed to them. They have to actively seek it out. In fact, a measure of performance in some organizations is your ability to acquire the information you need.

Understanding the framework of objectives for the company and all its components goes a long way toward minimizing confusion. The top executive should formulate specific objectives and the strategy for achieving them. He or she then has to communicate the pertinent parts to each operating unit, establishing with all of them their specific roles. Managers down the line sometimes have to take the initiative in getting a clear picture of what's expected of them.

Knowing the target is not enough for the manager who is interested in maximum contribution. It's sufficient only in highly bureaucratic organizations, where a person is merely holding claim to a specific "territory" and is expected to stay out of the way of others. The more a manager looks beyond his individual function, learns other points of view, and watches the effect of managerial decisions and actions on others, the more effective the manager can be in the job and in preparation for taking on broader responsibilities. The "any problem in the company is my problem" attitude is the sign of a manager with growth potential.

Experienced managers recommend that most of the information gathering be done through the system. It may be necessary to challenge the system from time to time, but don't set out to destroy it, they warn. The person you report to should be the source of much of the information you need, but things don't always work out that way. Many managers complain that the boss doesn't tell them enough: he's too lazy, or too busy, or he's jealous — or maybe he's standing ready to field any questions thrown at him.

Honest questions generally produce answers. If the boss doesn't have the information, an inquiry may prompt him to go after it. Eager subordinates should expect to run into some unknowns, however. The boss is probably smarter than they think he is, but he may have less information than they expect. Finding out that something is frankly not known can be worthwhile. It douses false assumptions and points up areas in which someone needs to develop information. When upper management openly admits that there are some questions without answers at the moment, that's not an excuse to rush down the halls rejoicing in the discovery of management incompetence.

If the boss is not providing enough information, a manager can turn to others — sometimes through informal conversations — and perhaps glean enough information to go back to the boss with an analysis and ask, "Is this the situation?" One young, top manager warns that if the boss then tells you it's none of your business, "the problem is more fundamental. You have to decide whether you're going to live with that situation or become a candidate for an executive search firm."

Not all research can be done through casual conversations. You may have to go more directly to the sources and ask for it. " Do the digging wherever the digging is needed," says another corporate officer, a man who has held executive positions in several companies. Looking back to his earlier days, he says, "I did it by making myself obnoxious. You've got to approach every person in a different way. If you dig to the best of your ability and still run up against blank walls, you're in the wrong company."

This willingness to face up to the possibility of leaving the company stresses the importance successful managers place on information. And they don't limit this to the information they "need." Some of them feel managers should have all the information they want because it furthers their understanding of the company and broadens their view for better performance and personal development. But they condemn those who leave their jobs dangling on the vine while gathering information only for the sake of grooming themselves for advancement. That's politicking.

Even legitimate information gathering can lead a manager into ticklish people relationships. It is sometimes met with opposition from executives far up the line, but experience shows that they will generally realize that it's better to work with a digger than try to fight. The individual who challenges the system and shows a commitment to something beyond selfish career advancement often finds that people will not slam the door. They may stand back, wondering what's up, and the manager may make some enemies along the way, but if it is clear that the information is being put to good use, he will possibly make some friends in the right places.

If the political situation becomes so hostile that it stifles the flow of information and cooperation, it's time to get out or to get rid of the politicians. Possession of information is a source of power, so efforts to acquire it lead to sensitive relationships. Honesty and openness can minimize the difficulties in the long run. They also make it easier for people to object to the time-waster who is merely satisfying an idle curiosity. After all, some of the people who are constantly plagued with the feeling that "nobody around here tells me anything" haven't earned the right to know.

MANAGER BY DAY, STUDENT BY NIGHT

Frank had a solid technical background. When he had the opportunity to become a product manager, a job with a heavy marketing slant, the need to step up his information gathering quickly became apparent. One of his first steps was to sift through indexes to periodicals, hunting for articles on general and marketing management. He then took a university course in financial management.

One of the toughest lessons for him wasn't in the books: learning to work within the business team and resisting the tendency to make unilateral decisions. As a new product manager, he knew little about customers' needs, personalities, products, and markets. He combed the company's literature and accompanied his salesmen on their calls. He also sought help from his boss, an experienced sales manager.

People who are serious about a career in management read and study. They examine the company's product information, policy statements, and organizational structure. They develop job-related skills such as writing, planning, and public speaking. They take self-study courses or enroll in universities to explore subjects such as accounting, economics, and organizational theory.

Structured learning reinforces on-the-job learning. If outside study relates to your work, it puts you into a mode for learning from what you are doing rather than moving mechanically through it. The work experience, in turn, provides some valuable final lessons to supplement classroom learning. For example, the study of interpersonal relations, psychology, and the behavioral sciences is valuable as background, but you have to experience the clash of personalities and cope with conflicting values and ambitions to know what managing is all about. A manager can't know how effective he is without trying to apply some classroom lessons within the real-world limitations that circumscribe the theoretical best.

Some classroom learning can and should be tested on the job. But not everything you should study will apply to what you are doing today, next week, or next month. For those management jobs up the line, there's never enough time to learn all that's needed. No matter when you start, you should have started sooner!

The pressures to cope with the infinite amount of learning have made the Master of Business Administration degree a popular route for people bent on careers in management. People coming directly from undergraduate studies and experienced workers bidding for accelerated upward motion trust that the curriculum will lay out the critical subject matter for them. Obviously, no university curriculum can include everything managers should know. And it can't give them the experiences of decision-making and risk-taking, despite the sophisticated game-playing built into some of the courses. The M.B.A. is not the only route into and through management, but its effectiveness in opening doors during the 1960's and 1970's can't be denied. From the company's point of view, the person with the M.B.A. has, at the least, passed an initial screening process demonstrating a reasonable intelligence and a commitment to a management career.

In 1950, only six universities offered this advanced degree. Today, almost 600 schools grant it. Nearly 50,000 students complete the requirements for the degree each year now. The M.B.A. — particularly from one of the prestigious schools — is a golden key to a better initial job than would otherwise be available. Some M.B.A. holders go far; many of them are in the upper ranks of management. But the degree wears thin if the holder does not have the right personality and experience for the top spots.

The degree has proved especially helpful to people with prior work experience — perhaps even some managerial experience. They find their effectiveness enhanced by adding theoretical knowledge to their real-world know-how. Some companies regard the M.B.A. holder as a fast-track person — one who will learn from work experience and move ahead quickly.

The person with an M.B.A. degree but no significant work experience first has to learn to adjust to the real task at hand. Theoretical "experience" leads too many young managers to believe they can handle tasks that they really aren't qualified for, say senior managers. Some suggest that the newly degreed person has been trained for a vice presidency but falls short of being qualified for lesser jobs. The case method of studying business problems "tends to make the students think in grandiose terms," says one corporate officer. "It is sometimes difficult for them to adjust to the workaday life of projects which are rather small portions of a corporation's activity."

Executives have complained that managers coming from the business schools are systems-oriented to the point of neglecting the people aspects of managing. They find that graduates who enter line rather than staff positions have the most difficult time making the transition from school to work because they have to deal with more people, their jobs are more action-oriented, and deadlines come faster.

The M.B.A. enables a person to be highly mobile. Dissatisfaction can set in rapidly, often within two years. Although the young manager's analytical input may be highly valued by some employers, the newly degreed generally doesn't command center stage in making decisions. Often, his or her recommendations are passed on to other managers, who assimilate them with other inputs and then make decisions that don't reflect the emphasis the contributor had in mind.

An M.B.A. can stimulate a management group. Older managers who may have heard of some of the qualitative and quantitative management techniques want their team to be able to employ them. The enthusiasm of the person newly equipped with these techniques can be contagious, too. Companies have found that force-feeding M.B.A.'s into their structures doesn't work as well as using them selectively as catalysts. Experience also suggests that the company should look at an M.B.A. holder not for his or her short-term capability but for long-term potential. The investment is risky; a dissatisfied M.B.A. is even more mobile than a happy one. The company has to be committed to making the investment pay off.

The ease of moving from academia to the world of work depends largely on the graduate's interpersonal skills. The capacity to interact with others is as important as the ability to think and solve problems. In an effort to avoid grinding out mere technicians, some of the graduate schools teach political organization theory and human nature theory. Devices such as team projects and discussion of classroom problems help break down singlemindedness and encourage an appreciation of other people's ideas and emotions.

Thousands of managers and would-be managers are enrolled in all sorts of courses through evening or weekend sessions at local universities, professional associations, or other institutions, including in-company schools. People also develop managerial skills through special assignments, such as study task forces and committee memberships. They grow through participation in community activities and professional and industry associations. Extracurricular "work" offers a chance to set and work toward goals, deal with new people, see new problems, learn other viewpoints, and practice new skills. Often, these activities can help them learn a great deal about themselves, since encounters with new situations and new people increase the number of interfaces for people to learn who they are and what is important to them.

Sandra Keifer, a charter member of Westinghouse Electric Corporation's "Campus America" program, found that volunteer work added a new dimension to her life. For her, it meant overcoming some of the disagreeable aspects of participating in the program as she addressed the nuclear power issue before college audiences across the country. (Her knees "shake like crazy" when she speaks in public.) She also had to work late nights and weekends to keep up with her regular duties as a nuclear engineer and manager of a mathematics and programming group.

Some companies offer paid leaves of absence for social service, government exchange programs, and education. As part of Wells Fargo Bank's personal growth program, employees may take several months' leave with full pay. The program is intended "to broaden the individual rather than add to his existing skills, and should enrich his personal attitude," says vice chairman Ralph J. Crawford, Jr., who conceived the program.

Whatever the motivations behind the leave-of-absence programs, relatively few people are permitted to participate. The programs may proliferate as people seek more avenues for fulfillment and as companies look for novel ways to spread out the workforce in times of slower economic growth. Since leaves of absence depend on having a flexible workforce and the ability to absorb the costs, however, these programs will be concentrated in the larger companies.

NOTHING BEATS A GOOD COACH

No aspect of management development — personal or institutional — offers as much leverage as good coaching by a supervisor. Because people seldom know what it is they need to learn, rarely see themselves accurately, and often can't see the impact of their actions on others, it helps to work closely with someone who can serve as a second pair of eyes. The boss can raise an individual's level of self-awareness, helping that person to more objectively analyze what he or she is doing, and how, as well as what the results are, and why. A good manager has a mixture of inborn and acquired skills and traits; effective coaching can help bring the favorable inborn characteristics to the surface, while directing the individual to the means for acquiring the necessary skills.

Environment, education, and experience shape a manager's development. The boss is usually the most important factor in that environment. To begin with, working for a good boss goes a long way in providing the incentive for doing well. An effective, coaching boss can guide the developing manager to the education courses that would benefit him or her most and provide the work experiences — long-term and special assignments — that will help the manager grow.

Not everyone is fortunate enough to have a boss who is good at coaching. Many young would-be managers have "failed" in their first positions because they did not get good coaching. When you report to a manager who is good in most areas of responsibility but weak or awkward in coaching, you are at a disadvantage. If you are observant and analytical enough, you can learn some things by watching to determine what the boss's style is, how it works, how decisions are approached, and what the results are.

You can't learn much from a boss who is just plain ineffective. You can try to observe what seem to be wrong decisions or the wrong ways to deal with people, but you may not be able to see all the wrongs or to deduce why things go wrong. The biggest drawback in working for a bad boss is that you will not be exposed to the strengths of good management. Poor managers are not the reverse image of good ones. Good managers get into more things that contribute to success than poor managers, and they avoid wasteful meanuevers. Working for a poor manager, you may not know what you're missing. You may also have to overcome the negative feelings you develop toward your boss, your work, and the company.

A good coach keeps in close touch with the manager, questioning and probing to analyze the subordinate's line of thinking, and keeping the manager on course. The coach should guide decision-making rather than step in and do things personally, and cultivate self-awareness by forcing the subordinate to think about what he or she is doing, and how, and what the results are. Decision-making and risk-taking are essential elements of managing that depend on the boss's willingness to delegate real problems. It's the successes and failures on the job that ultimately build management expertise. Making decisions requires an understanding of both the decision-making process and the facts that go into the process. Education courses or training programs may provide some of the information for some decisions, but the decision-making has to be practiced "under fire." Orientation or job-rotation programs have lost favor because they do not pin the individual down in a real learning situation; in these programs, you do not have to live with the long-term results of your decisions.

On-the-job learning, together with a good example to follow, represents the core of management development. The best a company can give a manager courageous enough to develop himself is the opportunity to learn and grow. This implies a willingness on the part of top management to take a risk and to tolerate mistakes — within reason, of course. If your boss's or your company's style is to jump hard on people who make mistakes, you're in a poor situation for learning. The manager who falls by the wayside isn't the one who makes mistakes but the one who can't learn from them. Companies looking for key executives have often put a lot of weight on the fact that a candidate may have been through a losing situation — assuming, of course, that they can be assured that this person has learned and grown as a result. The person who hasn't done anything wrong probably hasn't tried to do enough. At least that's the way effective top managers tend to look at people.

Managerial development isn't a passive process. The learner asks good questions and builds relationships with superiors, subordinates, and peers who can provide the information he or she needs to do the present job and to understand the broader implications of what's going on. Some managers have found it helpful to talk about management techniques and styles with the boss during formal appraisal sessions and with senior managers and peers on an informal basis.

"AM I FALLING BEHIND?"

"As a manager gets farther and farther up the line, the specifics of his responsibility become more and more general," notes the president of a large manufacturing firm. "He should do everything he can to divorce himself from the specifics of his old job and make sure he's got somebody in there who is going to be doing what he used to do. If he's a delegator and a manager, he should be depending upon other people to take care of those things." The effective manager cannot afford the luxury of spending too much time on the tasks of that former job. This means depending on others even when you feel you can do their jobs better than they can.

It's a rare manager who doesn't fear that he or she is falling behind when a job necessitates abandoning a well-known and loved specialty. In such cases, managers may feel they are throwing away years of study and experience. Suddenly you are spending more time dealing with people and organizations — and less time with the daily routine that was comfortable and maybe even fun. You not only need new skills and abilities, but your orientation must change. The higher managers rise, the broader their interests have to become. At lower levels, managers need to know the technology of their particular functions. At higher levels, they need greater mastery of business administration. They have to respond to and anticipate, if possible, the outside forces that affect their organizations.

When you are promoted to the multifunctional level, you may have to change styles. At this level, you can't plunge into problems the way you used to. You have to lean back and look at the entire situation. You have to overcome the tendency to develop a blind spot that prevents you from seeing the total problem — perhaps your original functional area or one toward which you have always felt uncomfortable.

As a multifunctional manager, you will discover — sometimes painfully — that you can't know as much as the people working for you do about the details of their jobs. If you do know one particular job better than a subordinate, you will grow rusty in time while the subordinate gets sharper. The more subordinates you have reporting to you, the less your chances are of being more expert at their games than they are. This fact of management life haunts managers with pangs of ineffectiveness. The successful ones realize they are paying people to know more about their specialties than they themselves know. They ask questions not only to learn the highlights of what is going on but to ensure that their subordinates are aware of the essential factors in the work they are doing. This healthy recognition of expertise also gives the subordinates a chance to feel good about educating the boss.

Some managers warn that it's possible to go overboard in pulling free from your old specialty. There is some value in maintaining your basic skills and keeping on top of major developments. While a manager strives to collect a team of people who are good resources, he or she may serve as one of the resources. Maintenance of some functional skill helps the manager understand new concepts and know if the staff is up to date. The manager who becomes too rusty cannot ask the right questions and may tend to reject good advice. What's worse, a "leader" may become dependent on people who are offering bad advice.

One top manager points out that moving upward can offer some advantages that permit you to "keep up" in a different way if you adjust your thinking. You stay abreast of the field by scanning — rather than reading in detail — the literature, and by associating with people who are in the forefront of that field. Rather than following the detail, you can get out in front and see the important trends and their implications.

The person who suffers too much anxiety over separation from a specialty may be handicapped for performance in the next job. At this point, such a manager should frankly consider whether any ambitions he or she might have about moving into more general management are realistic. The person suited for further upward motion finds intrinsic value and stimulation in new duties and may even welcome breaking away from functional detail.

Moving upward or not, managers can fall behind in other ways unless they keep growing. Managers may find themselves working with increasingly younger staffs whose attitudes, ambitions, and even style of dress may differ sharply from those of their managers. A change in corporate leadership may leave a manager behind, as far as the political structure or "the way we do things here" are concerned.

A rising manager can have some anxious moments when he looks ahead, too. Movement into the more general areas of management exposes a person to many fields in which he is a non-expert. Carl A. Gerstacker recalls how he had set his sights on a career at Dow Chemical Company and took a degree in chemical engineering. Later, as chairman of that company, he expressed regret at not having taken some courses in writing − to help in preparing reports and talks, in speech − to develop skills for the many public appearances he was called upon to make, and in political science − for his dealings with politicians. He also wished many times that he had studied literature, foreign languages, psychology, economics, sociology, and a host of other subjects that would have been invaluable in his career.

Moving upward in management invites feelings of falling behind in more and more areas of the business and in fields outside business. It's a fate the rising executive has to accept. If you can't − if you lack the enthusiasm and the energy to learn new things − you haven't got what it takes for the next job.

The manager who thinks he knows all that is necessary about himself, other people, the job, and the business is not doing the best job possible. That sort of attitude shortchanges the manager *and* the organization. When a manager stops learning, progress ceases; the effectiveness of the manager then begins to decline. What is worse, the inner self deteriorates.

GETTING IT ALL TOGETHER

The scope of management has broadened far beyond what appears to be the immediate job. It demands an understanding of the outside world and the manager's own inner self. The higher the corporate office, the more likely you are to find a person there who is not only on the leading edge in business matters but who is studying the arts, literature, nature, or some other area: a person with excitement about learning.

An effective executive must balance management science with art and humanity. The tools and techniques that sometimes are mistaken for the essence of management will work only in the hands of the man or woman who has integrated his or her whole life. The good judgment needed to find routes through complexity and ambiguity can only be built on solid character.

"Management is character as much as procedure, personality, or leadership style," says psychologist Frederick Herzberg of the University of Utah. This expert in organizational structure is impatient with people who look for simple prescriptions for management development.

As society places increasing emphasis on individual values and people insist on pursuing their wants rather than accepting those of a system, the effectiveness of corporate leadership will depend increasingly on what an executive is and what he or she believes. Tomorrow's managers will need the assurance of their own values and an appreciation for those which differ from their own.

The manager of General Electric Company's professional development operations agrees. "Know what you stand for and what you believe as you progress through various stages of your life," advises Dr. Lindon E. Saline. "That knowledge can give you the kind of freedom, personal security, and self-confidence that will allow you to lead an integrated life; to be open in all your feelings at home, in the office, and elsewhere."

4
The Heart of a Manager

At the highest corporate levels, three principal areas of resource management dominate executives' concern, says H. Robert Sharbaugh, recent chairman of Sun Company. They are: human, financial, and the hard-to-define combination of public affairs, policy, image, and constituency interface management. The first and third areas concern people relationships.

While first-line supervisors are obviously involved in people relationships with their workers, you might think that as a manager progresses upward he or she shifts from concentrating on people to concentrating on managing things or money. To the contrary, as Mr. Sharbaugh observes, top management has to tend to internal and external people relationships. Executives invest much time in that area of constituency interface management with employees, shareholders, customers, suppliers, government officials, and special interest groups.

The nature of management work in general may be clouded by the fact that there are many so-called managerial positions that do not involve managing people and depend on few, if any, people relationships outside the organization. A person may "manage" things — machinery, a set of accounting records, files, money — and yet may not be a manager. The "manager of shipping and receiving" may prove to be the guy on the loading dock who runs the lift truck. The "manager of accounts receivable" may work alone at a special and important operation. The term "manager" has been applied to many non-managerial jobs to upgrade their psychological compensations. Titles come cheap.

Yet management knows that the basic function of a genuine manager is to "get results through other people." At one time, a manager needed to be concerned with his ability to carry out instructions and be able to get others to do the same. But today people outside and inside the company — including managers themselves — want to understand why certain things are done; they want a "say" in how they are being done, too.

The basis for relationships has changed. Relationships depend more than ever on personality and character, even in this era of scientific management. That's why some top executives are convinced that managerial ability begins with *integrity* and *honesty* — character traits that are inborn or are developed early in the individual's environment. These qualities must not only be present but must be visible to others. If they rest beneath the surface and are not active, people find it difficult to act on what you say. People should feel that you have given them the whole truth. Their confidence in your fulfilling an agreement is based more on their feelings about you as a person than on anything else.

The best managers cast a positive aura. The traditional go-getter has generally been a fellow who is positive about who he is and what he wants, but the managers rising in today's humanistic setting go beyond that, to have a *positive attitude* toward other people, as well as toward themselves. Today's managers believe in people's potential to do good. They trust themselves and others; that accounts for their effectiveness in dealing with people. If you don't trust yourself, it's not likely you'll trust others; and if you don't trust people, you can't work through them or for them. If you do not possess this attitude by the time you reach management ranks, your ability to manage is limited. You will do better in a highly structured organization than in one which thrives on the free interchange of ideas.

THE "COOL" MANAGER

Since a manager has to focus people's thoughts and actions on certain objectives, he or she has to be genuinely interested in them, listen to them, and get the message across in terms that involve them in serving the organization's goals. *Sensitivity to people* is a more important character trait for a manager than raw intelligence or a wealth of business or technical data, believe most top executives.

"A manager must have the ability to give each person the human dignity that he needs," says one chief executive. "People have got to be convinced that whomever they're reporting to genuinely has their personal interests at heart, and that those are consistent with the interests of the company."

In a dynamic organization, a manager develops people, exercises their talents, and maximizes their effectiveness. The more humanistic the organization, the more the manager tries to maximize people as people and helps them raise themselves to levels of performance they may not have thought possible. A humanistic manager finds a common cause with others and leads them to action while learning their capabilities and wants.

Sensitive managers have a keen perception of the needs and desires of others even when they are not openly expressed. Therefore, they can frequently anticipate problems while the problems are still in the formative stage. They can sense the needs of their organizations and their supervisors, and they can detect the concerns of peers and subordinates that could get in the way of doing a good job.

Some managers have a special insight; call it *maze brightness.* You can't put your finger on it, but some people never find their way through the organizational subtleties, while others seem to succeed instinctively with a knack for learning who holds power, which secretary it is important to get along with, or exactly when to propose a new idea.

An effective manager appreciates the uniqueness of individual differences, points out an industrial psychologist. "He knows what makes people tick and reads people accurately and well. He probes inquisitively for reasons behind behavior instead of reacting to superficial and obvious characteristics. He is capable of showing both sympathy and empathy without being weak, gushy, or maudlin about it. He does not expect others to be carbon copies of himself. He encourages others to stretch their talents and grow as individuals."

Managers are often regarded as "cool" individuals – dispassionate, indifferent to people, with "ice in their veins." Today, they have to be "cool" in the updated sense of the word — recognize emotion-laden situations, do something worthwhile and live a meaningful life, and understand the problems of the people around them and be able to help.

The bull-of-the-woods manager who trods on people's feelings and demands instant obedience needs to control and be recognized as powerful. He may be able to get good results, particularly in lower management ranks, but over the long term, heel dragging is likely to be created among subordinates. The more the manager's position leads to exposure to people outside the corporation, the greater the chances of compounding trouble for the organization. The manager who is sensitive to the emotional content of people relationships has better chances of making smart decisions and winning cooperation in implementing them.

For the manager of the future, this represents a break from the tradition of screening people's emotions and feelings out of the decision-making process. The challenge now is to include the people factors and still take action, because the manager who is overly sensitive to people's feelings often becomes stalemated by their conflicting interests. The trick is not to go overboard in either sensitivity or insensitivity. A manager, therefore, is torn between "being very cold-blooded and objective" and " being so subjective that the company is not being run well," says Robert H. Malott, president and chief executive officer of FMC Corporation.

TO MANAGE IS TO RISK

Managing people implies a *willingness to take risks.* Working with others requires constant risk — especially when you go off and entrust a job to someone else. A manager makes a personal risk from the outset as he or she shares a commitment to the company and tries to win others to share it.

Management is a risk-oriented occupation. With an infinite number of potential actions to choose from, a manager must weigh the risks and benefits of each. Depending on the individual, the job, and the company, a manager may settle for courses of action that involve low risk and bring modest benefits, or seek those that are of high risk but carry the promise of high returns.

Although risk-orientation should be an important aspect of a manager's character, not all organizations require it of their managers. They sometimes permit the untested to rise through the structure without ever having to make an important, risky decision. When these people reach senior management ranks, where the ultimate responsibility for making decisions falls, the consequences are unfortunate for both the company and the individual managers.

Successful managers are also willing to take on risks in dealing with their bosses. They put their jobs on the line in order to do what they think the job demands. They will risk being fired, because, when things aren't right, they will either make changes or change jobs.

Pushing to explore his or her own potential, a manager will sometimes risk failure in order to learn. *Creativity* leads a manager to challenge habits, attitudes, and routine. But a good manager doesn't waste valuable creative energy on nonconformity in trifles such as hair lengths and dress codes. The more creative a person is, the more easily achieved is heightened awareness of some aspects of life by ignoring other aspects. And, since the aspects ignored are often precisely those routine matters on which an organization may dwell too much, this manager sometimes does not look like the ideal "organization man." In some organizations, conformity is valued more than creativity; conformity may be the style for "success" there.

A small percentage of managers are innovators. They generate many ideas and are willing to take risks to implement them. They are independent, directed from within. Some not-so-effective managers are rich with ideas; they tend to be dreamers rather than implementers of change. At the other end of the spectrum are people content to maintain past practices; they resist new ideas. These maintainers can play a role in certain jobs where control and stability are of prime importance, but too many of them can hobble an organization.

The majority of managers fall between these extremes. They are fairly strong at risk-taking and like to implement new ideas — their own or someone else's. They find satisfaction in bringing new concepts to life — a new product, a new production facility, a new organization. They know that innovative ideas do not become implemented solely by their own brilliance. Someone has to commit to them, make decisions, and act.

VALUES TO STEER BY

The person who is concerned primarily with protecting personal interests and advancing to a higher position will attempt to find a safe course of action. The truly effective manager tends to seek the right course rather than the course of least resistance. And that's seldom easy, since there may not be a "right course." A manager may have to compromise and negotiate in the midst of conflict and confusion. Thus, as a manager, your overall direction comes from your own values aided by an appreciation of the values of others. For the manager of the future, values beyond advancing oneself will be a must for success.

More and more companies realize they need managers who are well educated and broadminded enough to deal with values questions. They need leaders who can address the issues and answer criticism, since the broadening corporate role necessitates making value judgments and setting priorities. Managers are being challenged to reveal their human qualities. Increasingly, they have to relate what they are doing to the values in the surrounding environment.

Dehumanization of the workplace and of management until now has frequently forced managers to disregard what they personally believe — what's important to them. Despite the fact that this is the foundation on which a person employs his or her management expertise, subjects such as personal ethics, religion, and private ambitions have been taboo topics for discussion at work.

The management culture developed during this century has permitted only a rather antiseptic approach to values, morality, and religion. Partly in response to society's insistence that the corporation not interfere with the individual's spirituality, and partly due to scientific management's deemphasis of the human factors, managers have not had to deal openly with values and beliefs until recently. Now they encounter values issues on all fronts — with workers, with owners, and with the public at large.

Until now, perhaps the closest management has come to having a belief system or ideology has been in its support of free enterprise.

But relatively few managers have bound this into a coherent and consistent set of beliefs. It has often been a defensive posture, supported only by some vague notion of a hands-off system. Many managers have seen no connection between the freedom they want for their organizations and the freedom sought by employees and others. But fewer and fewer people, including managers themselves, are willing to subvert who they are for the sake of a job. The manager of the future will be as concerned about his or her own independence as anyone else.

Managers are not likely to hammer out a unified set of beliefs by which they will all operate. They will reflect the diversity of the society of which they are a part. As each expresses a coherent character, they will collectively undo the authoritative organization. In doing so, they will present themselves the task of dealing more and more with differing sets of values. They will need both boldness to assert new ideas, and compassion for the ideas of one another, if organizations are to have any meaning and be able to accomplish anything.

ROOM FOR BOLDNESS

There are many examples of one determined manager turning an organization around. The bold manager might not be the freewheeling, shoot-from-the-hip type who made a name for himself during the Roaring Twenties or the Soaring Sixties. He or she is more likely to be called "an innovator" or "an entrepreneurial manager." Boldness has been balanced with other attributes of a good manager.

Boldness alone can lead to trouble for managers and their organizations. Managers who ignore good advice, take poorly calculated risks, and fail to devise back-up plans in the event that things go wrong have slim chances of surviving. Today's bold managers have to be creative as ever, but they must rely heavily on information and opinion from others. Their boldness has to be tempered with risk analysis. They are measured not by their aggressiveness but by their effectiveness. The higher they rise, the better their risk analysis skills have to be, and the more sources of information and opinion they must be able to draw upon. Companies want professional managers who know how to acquire information and weigh it before making decisions. "We've seen aggressive people who cannot bring themselves to manage — or to accept management," says one chief executive. "They think movement and action are aggressiveness. A person has to be willing to fit into a management team if his aggressiveness is going to pay off."

On the other hand, some managers do all the right things up to the point of pushing for their conclusions. In one company, a particular manager was pushing top management for investment in a new line of products. After several years, the venture has still not borne fruit, but the promise remains. One member of top management says: "That manager will live to see the day when we will pat him on the back and say, 'You had a good idea.' " In the same company, another manager expressed misgivings about a new line of products. He stated his feelings but didn't fight hard against the idea; eventually, he flip-flopped and supported it. When the venture later failed, management remembered that "he was right in the first instance, but wouldn't stand up for his convictions."

Some managerial functions put a greater premium on boldness than others. A marketing executive, for example, is expected to constantly expand product lines and generate new ones, and to continually take personal and corporate risks. There are other positions for which a "maintenance manager" will fill the bill. Not everyone can be a bold manager, and too many in one organization can lead to instability.

One nationally known executive recruiter and management consultant believes that only about 20 percent of the top companies in the U.S. are actively seeking bold managers. Some top executives agree that, whether they do it intentionally or not, many companies discourage bold management by failing to solicit new ideas and not encouraging managers to speak up. Where control is too centralized, a manager may feel he or she doesn't have the freedom to push new ideas. Boldness comes in degrees, and many managers may be pressured into curbing this attribute. But the boldest will either take on the organization or leave it.

HOW MANAGERS SEE THEMSELVES

Rightly or wrongly, most managers perceive themselves as relatively bold. They are more likely to see themselves as dominating, bold, and self-assured than are other adults. In a series of extensive surveys, managers and administrative people differ most from others in scoring their own personality traits when it comes to "dominating." Nearly 51 percent of people in managerial-administrative positions think of themselves as dominating, compared with an average of 37 percent for all adults.* This feeling diminishes with age, however. The 18- to 24-year-olds in this group (of whom there are relatively few) are far more likely to feel dominant than are their peers. Among those of age 25 to 34, the frequency falls significantly; they are still more likely to feel dominant than are non-managers, but they are nearer the norm. The relationship remains about the same for 35- to 44-year-old managers. The percentage of managers who feel dominant rises again in the 45 to 54 range — the prime management age. Those in their final working years are far less likely to share this feeling; they're hardly any different from the non-managers by that time.

Today's young managers are far more likely to feel "brave" than are their non-management peers. They also feel braver than their elders do in the management ranks. As you go up the scale in age groups, however, both managers and non-managers give less and less indication of feeling brave.

Dr. Roger Gould, California psychologist and author of *Transformations,* has looked at this information and finds that it fits with his observations that managers shed some of their feelings of dominance with age. He explains: "The manager gets some sense of what he can't control, after some experience, and probably has less need to control as he matures." The effective manager learns that controlling and doing an effective job are not synonymous. With maturation, he realizes that things can be done without exerting direct control over them, and personal security and self-esteem

---

*Data on self-perceptions has been drawn from the Target Group Index surveys — national product and media studies owned by Simmons Market Research Bureau, based on interviews with more than 30,000 adults a year.

permit the manager to "let go." Dr. Gould continues: "In your twenties, you're bluffing most of the time. You need all these props. But they are interferences. They're posturing. As you become more of a decent human being you can become less brave, less dominating."

Feelings of self-assuredness is where managers are next most likely to differ from non-managers in the way they perceive themselves. A successful manager generally will gain self-assuredness and feel less need to prove himself. On the other hand, a manager in an uncomfortable situation may lose ground; he or she may feel that it is necessary to display bravery or to act in a domineering manner. This manager may need the "props" more than ever.

The managers most likely to regard themselves as "awkward" are those in the 35 to 44 age range. They are coping with additional responsibilities and are being thrust into new areas of knowledge — or ignorance. Surprisingly, in these years, when they are beginning to "arrive," they are less likely to perceive themselves as dominating, self-assured, brave, broadminded, or intelligent than are younger managers. These early or middle management years are humbling. This is a low point for feeling amicable, efficient, and creative. Yet the challenge must agree with many of these managers, since fewer feel tense than do younger managers. They are also much less likely to feel tense than are non-managers of the same age.

In the middle decade of management — age 45 to 54 — the manager seems to shed some awkwardness; in fact, this is the least awkward time in a manager's career. Now he is really rolling and is more likely to think of himself as kind, broadminded, efficient, amicable, and creative. Yet the same manager is a little more likely to be tense, to insist on feeling dominant, and to slip in self-assuredness. While many of these people are in powerful positions, the narrowing of the pyramid can be seen. They may not make it to the top. And even if an individual doesn't care about that, the question remains: When am I going to peak out or be shoved out? Along with power has come vulnerability.

By age 55 to 64, the manager is in a smaller group that includes the few persons at the helm of their company, some in key corporate offices, department and division chiefs, senior staff persons, and middle managers who are still hanging on. This mixed group is more apt to admit to feeling awkward than are the 45- to 54-year-olds. They also back off on some of the attributes that seem essential to good management — perhaps a sign of their mellowing. They are more likely to feel kind, frank, and amicable. They are less inclined to feel brave, dominant, intelligent, or creative.

Sometimes, in the later years, managers see their power diminish. "Self-assurance goes down with diminishing power and with age," says Dr. Gould. One of the occupational hazards of being a manager, he says, is encountering that "sort of smothering that takes place in an organization unless you're at the very top."

CUTTING THROUGH THE FOG

Managers who get to the top or who are on their way there are distinguished by their *willingness to make tough decisions.* Most people like to make easy decisions but prefer to duck the tough ones even if they are capable of making them. Because of their commitment and their desire to achieve, strong managers are willing to face up to a decision and make it even if there is a good chance of being wrong.

The willingness to make decisions can grow through experience, and the quality of your decisions can improve if you learn from that experience. There are, of course, people who repeatedly make bad decisions; they are not managerial material. The trick of good decision-making is to get all the good input you can before making the choice, managers advise. The more you know about a problem, the more options you give yourself for solving it. Make the decision. Acknowledge that it is too late for second thoughts. Go on to the next task. Come back at some later time to analyze what was accomplished, what went wrong, or what could have been improved.

The ability to solve problems can be a wasted asset unless you have the *ability to set priorities.* This requires that you be free from bias and possess enough emotional maturity to put first things first. It also requires knowing what your objectives are. This is where top management can help; in the early stages of your development, it should provide priorities in detail and impress upon you that, as you grow in your job, you are expected to be able to set your own priorities. Then, if you are going to become an effective manager, you develop an understanding of the value of time and the need for establishing priorities for the expenditure of it.

A manager's time frame changes as he or she progresses upward. Both the interest and the capacity to think more and more about the future are needed. Without *future orientation,* a manager would neglect the vital function of setting goals and fail to consider all the possible problems and opportunities on the horizon. An organization adds up to little more than a collection of short-term results with no insurance of long-term viability unless someone imparts a spirit or direction to give it vitality. The ability to recall historical information about the company, the business, etc. can improve chances of making a good decision by putting it into better perspective. It also has a way of instilling confidence in superiors and subordinates. They are less apt to worry that some of the mistakes of the past are going to be repeated. They may even sense that there is a perspective at work that encompasses not only the past but the future.

Unfortunately, managers are often put under pressure to serve the short term rather than the long term. If managers want to demonstrate their effectiveness, it can most easily be done by improving the score right now. For example, a general manager can reduce advertising expenditures, trim research and development spending, cut corners on replacing old equipment, and spend less on employee training. By diverting these investments in the long-term future, he can make quick improvements in the profit picture. Some managers do this when quick improvement is imperative; others use such tactics to make themselves look good so they can quickly move up to another rung on the corporate ladder (and let someone else inherit the problems they have sown). These tactics can impress both supervisors and investors. Another manager may spend months restructuring his or her organization, staffing it with better people, weeding out inventories of obsolete goods, and investing in the development of new products. The quarterly earnings report may be every bit as bad as the manager expected, but others interpret it only as a sign that the organization is going downhill.

The variety of time considerations facing managers test their adaptability. They often find themselves worrying about five-year plans and the year's budget, as well as this week's deadlines. They struggle to serve several masters at once. The conflict between the present and the future can be charged with tremendous emotion. Take the case of David Kimball, president and chief executive officer of Leeds and Northrup Company when that company was trying to evade the clutches of Tyco Laboratories, Inc., and others in 1978. He was constantly forced to look over his shoulder to see who was in pursuit and how close they were getting. It would have been easy to abandon the long-term essentials such as long-range planning, technology assessment, market research, and organizational development — the kinds of tasks that require "fairly long unbroken concentration" for up to eight hours at a time. "One of the most important things was not to change the fundamentals of the general business plan or the long-range plan," he says. It is sometimes difficult to maintain that posture because you also have to meet some short-term objectives or there won't be a tomorrow.

Planning ability is one of the toughest tests of a manager's character. He or she has to stick to the original plans when the going gets tough and yet be willing to change them to match changing conditions. Good managers evaluate the results of their actions, learning as they go. They question the "normal" solutions to problems and the solutions they previously chose, continually asking if there isn't some totally different approach. They appreciate trade-offs, finding seemingly unrelated factors that can present a totally new route to a solution.

People who can draw up good plans, and even those who can adapt plans and make them better, are not necessarily good managers. A manager has to communicate the objectives of the plans and get people involved in attaining them. Since a company generally has numerous objectives, some of which conflict with others, a good manager has to simplify them and bring them into harmony. "You have to reiterate them frequently, and it is important not to tack violently," adds Mr. Kimball.

In the postwar years, managers have become increasingly sophisticated at planning. Many have learned to develop long-range plans and strategic plans. Some consider alternative futures with an extremely distant horizon. But, above all, management has learned that there is no such thing as a "foolproof plan."

With the number of unknowns increasing, and their interrelationships compounding, a manager must be able to act decisively even when not 100 percent sure of the outcome, or when not totally convinced that plans won't have to be modified somewhere down the road. Managers — especially top executives — need a high *tolerance for ambiguity*.

As the world changes and the corporate response and structure change along with it, even the manager's closest relationships become ambiguous. A manager may find that he or she is not clearly "the boss"and, in turn, has to follow someone who is not clearly the boss. Areas of management responsibility are broadening and overlapping; more people are affecting the plans. Therefore, the manager who has been taught to be competitive finds that effectiveness often requires a *willingness to collaborate*. He or she must proceed with no prescription for what to do, how to do it, or who is to do it. Despite the ambiguities, a good manager conveys a positive aura that encourages others to join in attacking the unknown.

5
What Worries Managers Most

For all their effectiveness on the job or in other activities they may pursue, managers do not stride along totally free of personal and professional worries. Bold as they are, they have doubts. Successful as they may be, they have regrets and anxieties. Very human factors drive them to do some things well and sometimes detract from their being fully effective.

In a 1978 survey by *Industry Week* magazine, several hundred managers were asked to list their chief worries from each of three categories: personal, workplace, and national. The survey revealed that they worry most about their children, their health, career stagnation, the quality of their company's products, inflation, and government regulation.

Most managers are not worried about their abilities. What they do worry about is getting the opportunity to employ their skills, to have their abilities recognized, and to meet high standards despite the many demands on their time.

PERSONAL CONCERNS COME FIRST

There's an all-too-familiar image of the self-centered executive whose children barely know him and whose devotion to them is expressed only through the checkbook. The *Industry Week* survey rejects that image. Thirty percent of the managers said their children are their principal worry. Perhaps they are frustrated by seemingly futile attempts to pass on "traditional" values or the fear that what their children have learned at home is being undermined on the outside. The standards that they have lived by are in conflict with the standards of their children or, at least, those of their children's peers. These managers may feel, too, that they have been less successful as parents than as workers. In many cases, while a man may have been influential at work, he feels he has fallen short in being a shaping influence at home. Unfortunately, says one manager, "neither work demands nor children demands fit themselves nicely into a specific time slot."

Career-oriented mothers face a special child-rearing problem, divided as they are between the desire to work and the desire to provide the best home for their children. But one mother says, "Working makes me a better person, and as such I can make a better home for my child and husband. When others criticize me for working and leaving the baby with a sitter, I explain to them that there are many mothers who hate being home and want to work. They aren't good mothers as a result."

Despite today's high incidence of divorce, most of the managers responding to the *Industry Week* survey apparently are not troubled by their marriages. Although 95 percent of them are married, only 8 percent mentioned their marriage as their primary personal worry. The marriage relationship did not show up strong even in the naming of their top three worries.

A fourth of the survey respondents ranked their own health as their number one personal worry. In fact, most managers gave health some ranking among their personal concerns. Work and health pose a delicate balancing act for managers. The nature of their work does not always contribute to good health; for some, it is damaging. Yet their effectiveness depends on good health. They cannot afford to have even a minor ailment hamper their performance by raising their anxiety, kindling fears, or filing a hair trigger on their tempers. Those managers who have been through life-threatening physical setbacks say the impact can remain long after the real physical disability has passed. Even those who enjoy good health are concerned because they don't adhere to regular exercise programs, don't relax enough, or don't eat properly, and suspect that eventually their ways will catch up with them. Realizing that good health is basic for good performance on the job, they are frustrated because involvement in their work gets in the way of following rules of good health care.

Another major personal worry centers on the pace of career advancement — or lack of it. Young managers may be bothered by the threat of a career standstill. Those nearing retirement complain of being put out to pasture; to them, the termination of their corporate ascent came as a powerful blow. Older managers worry about retirement — having enough money and filling their free time with enjoyable and stimulating activities. The less exciting their careers have been, the greater the danger that retirement will be confining and dull. Young managers are sometimes concerned about retirement, but primarily in terms of giving long-range consideration to setting aside some money for those distant years.

WORKPLACE WORRIES

Concern about the company's product ranks highest among managers' work-related worries. Even when they feel their product quality is first-rate, they worry about keeping it that way. Concern turns to anxiety if they feel they cannot control the factors that determine quality. They may blame workers who do not take pride in their work. They may feel the boss is to blame, and that's even more frustrating. Many managers with ulcers blame them on a boss who couldn't make a decision or who zig-zagged in direction. Frustration over inability to alter the situation, combined with the fear that it is endangering his future, may tear away at the manager's health.

When a person feels he or she has some control over a situation, there may be less of an inclination to worry about it. A whitecollar worker who repeatedly showed signs of stress during his annual physicals was promoted into management, and his next physical showed marked improvement in his condition. The doctor pointed out that, despite the added responsibility, the manager was now in a position to act rather than watch and churn. Several studies have shown that managers suffer less from stress-related, psychosomatic ailments than do bluecollar workers. While both groups may be under stress, the manager may be able to minimize the deleterious effects by being in a position to attack the sources.

Deadlines can keep managers worrying no matter how much they enjoy tackling the problems before them. Nearly half of all the *Industry Week* survey respondents listed "meeting deadlines"as one of their principal workplace worries, and one out of six ranked it number one. Meeting the deadlines is only part of the problem — perhaps just the tip of the iceberg. For the most part, managers take pride in their ability to meet their targets, but regret that deadlines prevent them from doing the best job possible, forcing them to act with inadequate information, jeopardizing the quality of their work, and blocking them from cooperating with others in a way that would contribute to a more effective overall operation.

One of the common work-related concerns for managers is the long-term prospect of inflation. Not all managers work in positions that are directly affected by external business conditions, but few can escape the very real impact inflation has on the way they operate. Fast-rising prices may raise the degree of risk in their business decisions. Long-range investment plans are complicated by the fact that equipment prices increase substantially between the planning stage and completion. Sales made on long-term contracts may not be priced high enough to cover future cost increases. Granting wage and salary increases becomes an extremely delicate balancing of cost control versus fairness to workers whose real incomes are shrinking. Inflation is more than a business factor — it is a real worry with human dimensions.

FRUSTRATED BY REGULATION

The continual intrusion of government deeper and deeper into business affairs has been a mounting concern for managers over the past two decades. Outside pressures that have been transformed into government regulations force managers to be defensive, conservative, and pessimistic when they should be action-oriented, future-oriented, and creative. They feel they are expected to pursue new ideas aggressively, be open to new ways of doing things, and take business risks that will result in better lives for all; therefore, they feel betrayed by this climate that entices them to inaction, short-term results, and conformity.

There is hardly a manager at any level, in any function, in any company, who is not affected by regulatory activity in his or her daily work. While management generally sympathizes with the goals of the regulations — fair employment practices, a cleaner environment, health and safety, and other objectives that they support as individuals — they are frustrated by the means used. Some, in fact, are especially frustrated because, from where they stand, they can see the goals being jeopardized by actions which may not really be serving the public. The worst aspects of the situation are the duplication, inconsistencies, continual tinkering, an overload of reporting, and the adversary attitude of many regulators.

While old guard managers may see regulations as an invasion of their turf, the modern manager objects on the grounds that the regulations are obstructing his delivery of solutions. The latter is not troubled by being expected to do too much but by not being permitted to do what's expected. A multi-billion-dollar paperwork jungle drains off manpower and attention from more productive and meaningful activities. Managers see no way to be aware of and comprehend all the pertinent requirements and resolve all the conflicts set up by the federal, state, and local agencies.

In the auto industry, executives work at resolving several objectives simultaneously: reducing pollution, conserving fuel, improving safety, and holding costs in check. Ford Motor Company's Bennet E. Bidwell wonders if, in its rush forward, the industry is truly serving the public. There is a tradeoff between cleaning up the air to a given level by a given time and improving fuel economy, he says. "I think we have done a poor job of asking the public which way it would vote, given the alternatives and the costs involved."

Complicating the issue is government's penchant for not only mandating objectives, but also for detailing, or at least strongly implying, methods to achieve them, says Mr. Bidwell, who is Ford's vice president, sales group, North American Operations. "When that happens, you begin to lose something called freedom of choice."

The solutions detailed in regulations are based on present knowledge (or lack of it) and present capabilities. Responsible managers would prefer to reach out for new solutions, since this is the nature of their job and the role of business. How an industry goes about meeting national objectives "ought to be our business, because our business is going to succeed or fail on whether we do it in a way that's acceptable to the public," says Mr. Bidwell. "To me, the overriding question is at what point does big government break the productive back of this country. Today, gradually, the people who produce, engineer, or drill, or mine, or sell are becoming an extinct species."

Compliance with regulations, record-keeping and reporting threaten to dampen managers' motivation. For the most part, they aren't sinking under the weight of it. Many have come to accept it as part of the job. For some, however, it has destroyed the job. A corporate vice president takes early retirement because the hassle has turned a career into a grinding chore. A research and development manager leaves for a university post in hopes of finding an unfettered work climate. The company's environmental control director, who took the job with drive and confidence, turns sour and cynical. Hourly workers have been known to decline promotions to supervisory ranks because they don't want to get involved in the regulatory mess.

Older managers are concerned that the new generation entering the management ranks, who have never operated in an unencumbered system, may yield too much to overregulation. Not all the young managers like the system, however. Many of them feel thwarted in their efforts to respond to new objectives set for the corporation. Because they are so strongly in favor of many of the basic aims of the regulations, they are especially disappointed by government's maze of conflicting rules and mountains of meaningless paperwork which get in the way of attaining these aims, often becoming ends in themselves. But, says one of them, "we do have a higher threshold of frustration than older managers." Younger managers are, perhaps, a little more willing to work with the regulators and are more optimistic that the system can eventually be made reasonable and effective.

Corporate managers will have to walk the line between frustration and defeatism, on one side, and capitulation to unreasonable demands, on the other. If, in frustration, they take a strictly defensive position, they will be swept under. If they capitulate, there will be no one to tend to the problem-solving sector and no one to prevent worthy goals from being smothered by procedure. Humanagement offers to bring business and government into a balance that serves society's needs. As it fashions organizations that are responsive, the public may then demand significant pruning of the jungle of overregulation to allow the corporation to get the job done.

LAW SUITS AND JAIL SENTENCES

The manager who doesn't respond to the realities of the world outside the corporation places himself in jeopardy. There was a time when an executive or middle manager could feel safe behind the company gates. Whatever was done in the course of performing a job was generally regarded as an action of "the company." If someone suffered harm resulting from that activity and decided to sue for damages, he or she would sue the corporation. If a government agency found evidence of unlawful conduct, it would sue the corporation.

But times have changed. You still can't send a corporation to jail. But you can send the company president, chairman, a member of the board of directors, or even a plant manager or superintendent to jail. You can sue them for everything they're worth — and then some. It's a consideration that injects a high degree of personal risk into the manager's normal risk-taking assignment.

Since plaintiffs in damage suits are going after the people responsible as well as that inanimate creature called "the company," companies are quickly learning to provide insurance coverage to protect their top executives and directors against personal financial loss. But liability isn't limited to the people at the top. The upper-echelon executive has to worry not only about his or her own performance; but being accountable for the mistakes, misdeeds, and negligence of employees down the line.

As Congress and state legislatures have generated a growing mountain of regulatory law, the exposure of top executives to criminal liability has grown correspondingly. They can encounter charges steming from violations of securities law, antitrust law, occupational health and safety regulations, pension plan requirements, laws prohibiting employee discrimination, and product safety regulations, to name a few. Managers feel especially vulnerable to damage claims if they are responsible for overseeing pension funds. A company official, acting as a fiduciary for a fund, could face damage claims simply for making an improvident investment with these monies. It's not a matter of mismanagement or fraud. Liability can be incurred through honest errors in judgment.

Although unethical conduct is the cause of trouble in a minority of cases, it provides the impetus for many of the laws and regulations now in place and the excuse for still more. "Considering all the instances in which corporate leaders have violated minimum standards of ethical behavior, it is understandable that there should be so much pressure for the regulation of corporate conduct," says Fred T. Allen, chairman and president of Pitney-Bowes, Inc. But, he points out, most of the cases of unethical conduct violated existing laws or regulations; they did not point to the need for piling up more legislation and regulation.

CORPORATE ETHICS DEPEND ON PERSONAL ETHICS

Mr. Allen recommends that managers take steps to ensure that the conduct of business reflects the highest ethical standards. This means weighing short-term opportunities against the "moral price." It also means top management has to reassure its employees that ethical conduct is mandatory; this can be aided by setting business objectives that are not so unrealistically high as to imply that anything goes in reaching them. He also maintains that businessmen must speak out for corporate morality to change the assumption of the minority of businessmen that unethical or marginal behavior is the necessary price of doing business. Along with this goes supporting just penalties for violators.

A survey of *Industry Week* readers shows that 80 percent believe ethics in industry have not slipped and may actually be improving. These managers claim, too, that their own conception of right and wrong defines proper business behavior, not company policies, society's expectations, or anything else.

"Managers quite properly are no longer satisfied to accept any idea 'just because the boss says so.' They want to know the reasoning, think it through, and test its soundness for themselves."

Those are the words of J. Irwin Miller, who headed Cummins Engine Company for many years — an executive who set an outstanding example of ethical business behavior. He has stressed that "top management must make clear that people at all levels are responsible as individuals, that concerns and questions of appropriate conduct will be listened to, and that the company is interested in the means rather than simply the end."

Many executives agree that ethics can't be decreed within a company any more than they can be legislated by government. They can be stated. They can be discussed. But ultimately they must come from within the individual. In this time of individualism, changing values, and diverse lifestyles, that would seem to open a Pandora's box of unethical behavior. A truly humanistic setting, however, is based on ethics — on fairness, honesty, and mutual respect. Diversity and individuality quickly die out unless they are exercised within ethical standards. The corporation that is humanized in its objectives and its methods can draw unprecedented power from the richness and diversity of its people.

"We don't have a code of ethics because we think they tend to be platitudes that can lull you into thinking the matter is taken care of once and for all," said William H. Wendel when he was president of Carborundum Company. "I don't think you can create ethics by proclamation, but I do think a company is a culture and the pattern of that culture is set by example at the top," Mr. Wendel added.

Codes of ethics make sense if you make them a living document. Armco Steel Corporation first laid out its "Armco Policies" in 1919 because it felt "you should put down on paper what you expect of others and what they could expect of you," chairman C. William Verity has explained. "These policies will have a real value only so long as others believe they are alive and that management is going to abide by those policies," he insists. They are a "mutual commitment." Armco holds courses in the interpretation of the policies for its supervisors. Every new employee receives a copy of them and an explanation of what they mean.

The Armco example further underscores the importance of making ethics a personal matter. There is no substitute for personal standards. The best a company or a manager can do is to sensitize people to ethical considerations. Some top managers in industry do this by meeting with key managers and posing hypothetical ethical questions for discussion. The result may be no clear-cut, agreed-upon, standard answer for future reference. But managers who have been through the exercise are more likely to consider the ethical questions posed by actual "business" situations.

Increased legislation to control business behavior might lead people to figure that anything that is not prohibited by law is ethical. Taking too much responsibility away from the individual lessens the power of personal ethics. Ironically, the regulatory burden may already be encouraging dishonesty and unethical conduct, some managers point out. For example, some people simply cannot meet the paperwork requirements. When a corporate staff member calls a supervisor with an exhaustive list of questions for a government form, he or she may be told "just put down anything." Or, if someone has a report due in a few days that requires top management attention when the senior executives are out of town, he or she simply fills it out.

ANXIETY AS A CONSTANT COMPANION

A whirlwind of conflicting demands, high expectations, and severe limitations make it difficult for managers to act. Legal and ethical considerations raise the level of complexity still higher — beyond what managers have had to manage. We are in an age of complexities and uncertainties which defy risk analysis. As a result, "business executives have come to know anxiety as a constant companion," says social analyst Daniel Yankelovich. "The normal worry or fear associated with known risks has been compounded by anxiety over unknown factors. As executives, we put our skills on the line, deciding what factors will make the difference between failure and success. We measure such risks as carefully as possible, but today we often don't even know what to measure."

People can be comfortable with some uncertainty; they become uncomfortable if there is none at all, say psychologists. But, says Mr. Yankelovich, "the amount of stimulation and change — of uncertainty — threatens to become intolerable." The manager has difficulty maintaining his or her stability and control.

People choose their careers, to some extent, on the basis of their tolerance for ambiguity and anxiety. Those with a low threshold seek refuge in simple tasks or numbers-related occupations where things seem solid and clear. Others, and especially upper managers, have a high tolerance for risk but "an acute need to control the forces that make any decision risky," says Mr. Yankelovich. "Most of the tools of the managerial trade are designed to measure and control risk factors, and the professional manager is by temperament a person who fights to limit risk. Ironically, this renders him less tolerant of uncertainty. The stronger a person's need to be on top of things, the more likely he is to be susceptible to the anxiety of uncertainty. Today's executive tends to rely upon quantification, systematic thought, priority-setting, and tightening the lines of control . . . . Statistical-control skill has become, in many companies, the test of executive competence."

When uncertainty threatens your need for control, you may respond out of anxiety rather than sound judgment. Mr. Yankelovich describes five possible responses to anxiety:

1. Denying or avoiding things which make you uncomfortable.
2. Taking action just for the sake of taking action.
3. Shifting the decision-making responsibility from yourself to the group.
4. Projecting your anger onto others so that your anger appears to be their anger; displacing your own sense of disorder upon the world so that it looks like the world is coming apart.
5. Working harder and longer and putting pressures on others.

How can you avoid making responses from weakness? Mr. Yankelovich suggests that you first recognize that you are suffering from anxiety, that you have passed your tolerance for uncertainty. You should then discuss your anxiety with someone – a colleague, a friend, or an outsider – who can act as a sounding board.

The next suggestion from Mr. Yankelovich meshes with much of the current literature that runs counter to what managers have been taught. Give the right hemisphere of your brain a break, he says. The left hemisphere controls logical, orderly, rational, verbal, analytical thinking – the substance of management science, if you will. The right hemisphere sees patterns, grasps things as a whole, or knows intuitively. The left hemisphere works best under conditions of normal risk, he says. Dealing with uncertainty or the unknown does not lend itself to mechanical, computer-aided, logical problem-solving. But the anxiety it creates tempts you to lean harder and harder on the left side when you should be trying to find ways to open yourself up to new possibilities and ways of perceiving things. While the physiology of right hemisphere/left hemisphere roles has not been resolved, Mr. Yankelovich's call for the addition of a fundamentally different approach to problem-solving remains valid.

As the science of management has risen, the critical problems facing management have become non-scientific, non-quantifiable. The technological options available to managers are only part of the complexity they face. Their role is to serve diverse values and multiple relationships in a world that is becoming both more personal and more global. They can fill it only by investing more of their total person in their work. They must practice humanagement − not mere management. The rise of humanagement does not imply abandonment of rational thinking but a blending of science and logic with humanity and art. It depends on special people who can understand computer printouts but refuse to let them overrule good human judgment and imagination.

6
The Myth of Perfection

Managers live with ambiguity. Some thrive on the challenge of doing the best they can against undetermined odds. But many try to shield themselves and their organizations from ambiguity with procedures and systems. They hide behind a mask of perfection to avoid anxiety-causing situations, screen out their personal feelings, avoid discussing differences of opinion, and compensate for the lack of legitimate means of instilling confidence in others.

Over a long period of time, this effort has been institutionalized, leading some people to believe that the system is right, that the procedures are infallible, and that the managers who implement them are unerring. Newcomers to management can easily fall victim to the notion that only the perfect rise to the top and that the only wrongs are due to human failure to fit the system.

A manager may know more than his or her employees about what has to be done and why. But not always. Managers are generally right in assuming they know more about what is going on; after all, they should have better sources of information. But they have no monopoly on knowledge or wisdom. They can only give that pretense if they put on the mask of perfection. But in so doing, they lessen their effectiveness in the long run by ignoring both what people have to offer and the imperfections that will foul up their systems. A "proper" system will not override the irrationalities that play within and between people. And it will not cover up the manager's own imperfections.

Wise managers know that neither they nor a select group have all the right answers. One executive admits that he once thought that 10 percent of the people have 90 percent of the ideas and get 90 percent of the work done. The secret to his job, he thought, was to sort out the effective 10 percent. But he has learned that talent and ability are much more broadly distributed. The wise manager knows, too, that there is no such thing as "the right answer" in many cases. The choices available to him are more likely to be "the least of the possible evils," "the most practicable," "the most popular," "the most expeditious," and "the best for the long-term," but not one that is "absolutely right."

People with whom any manager deals are rightfully skeptical when the manager feels he or she is absolutely right, and they can be unforgiving when a manager is wrong. The public is offended by the finality with which a corporate executive may answer — or decline to answer — questions that are of vital interest to them. The mask invites suspicion and keeps people at arm's length. When people see behind it, they are encouraged to prove the manager wrong any time they can.

Humanagement strips away the myth of perfection. It does not require the manager to be superior or even to act superior. It permits managers to offer themselves as resources for enabling others to help *them*selves. It does not compel managers to pretend that neither they nor their organizations have no problems. You do not have to be unerring in order to lead. Revealing your own humanity not only lets you be yourself, it can help get the job done. Admitting a mistake, showing a sense of humor, or sharing a doubt cements stronger relationships than does a "perfect system" or a "perfect person."

People like systems not only because they help ensure a continuity of operations but because they reduce the need to make decisions by establishing rules to guide action. Sometimes these routines can guide people to stupidity. Take the case of the Eastern manufacturer that bought special paper for packaging its sensitive electrical products. No one knew why; everyone just assumed that the high-cost paper was essential for protection during shipment. Until, that is, one purchasing executive scrutinized the matter and discovered that years ago, the "special" paper was nothing more than a neighboring firm's waste, purchased at rock-bottom prices. When that firm went out of business, a new supplier was found — at a much higher price.

THE POWER OF PERSONALITY

An effective manager knows that people are more powerful than a system. Motivated and led in the right direction, they can accomplish far more than people slaving to a pre-planned system. Turned off or antagonized, they can tear a system apart.

Time and again, individual managers have shown they can produce better results than can a carefully designed organization with all its policies and procedures. Sometimes one person can turn an organization around. The value of one good executive was dramatized in 1978, when Lee Iacocca moved from Ford Motor Company to the presidency of Chrysler Corporation. People were astonished to hear that Chrysler was spending several million dollars to cut the strings still attached to Iacocca after Ford fired him. But Chrysler was convinced that his know-how and image would make that investment pay off many times over.

On the other hand, small irrational decisions can affect the organization as much as formal, calculated, executive decisions. The uncertainties of the future, people's unexpected emotional reactions, and the manager's own imperfections and emotions defy any system that has been devised. Yet the mainstream of management practice up to now has been to devise systems that closely regulate functions and people. Ironically, the weaker the manager, the more he or she relies on the system — on "policy."

For years, managers have been taught that decisions should be made unemotionally. Some have construed this to mean they should bar emotional factors — their own and others — from the decision-making process. Unfortunately, emotions and feelings do come to play and can make the best of intentions fail. Managers are now coming to realize that they cannot manipulate people to achieve their goals simply by being "objective." A manager's own personality is a key determinant in obtaining his or her objectives. People's reactions to a manager are critical. The negative reaction of a worker, customer, or member of the community can bring brilliant plans to humiliating defeat.

Likewise, managers can see that sharing their hopes and excitement may spur people to turn a modest plan into a great success. Effective humanagement comes from controlling your emotions, not from denying them. A manager may let it be known, for example, that he is angry, but he cannot afford a temper tantrum that will shatter people's confidence in him. For the same reason, a manager has to control any tendencies toward moodiness. Since part of the job is to build the spirits of others, a manager's melancholy or ambivalence can dampen managerial effectiveness. People cannot follow managers who are the type about whom they are forced to say, "I thought I understood him but I don't." John Dwyer, president of American Seating Company, says: "If one of my managers were to have a hot temper, he would be unpredictable. And as chief executive officer, I have to have predictability in my people. I have to know that if a manager says something, he means it. Temper is a destructive thing because it shuts off the lines of communication."

If a manager doesn't appreciate the emotional content of a situation or realize that the emotional reactions to a decision are as important as the bare facts that go into the making of it, he or she is inviting trouble. "Ninety percent of all managers don't recognize emotional content when confronted with it, and they really aren't to blame because our culture simply does not teach us to respond to emotion but rather to facts," says one industrial psychologist.

Humanagement gives full weight to people as people – emotions and all. It is based neither on demands that they be perfect nor that they be so limited in freedom of action that they can do little wrong – or right. Organizations of the future will harness immeasurable power by unharnessing people, giving them full value *as people.*

CHEAP TRICKS WITH COSTLY IMPACT

Lack of respect for people can be revealed in seemingly insignificant actions that can have significant negative impact. For example: each weekday morning, one high-level executive strolls into his headquarters building, purchases a newspaper, and ascends to his office. He proceeds to read his paper carefully, and then, with equal care, folds it, and hands it to his secretary. She has come to dread what follows. She marches to the newsstand, hands the paper back to the clerk, and asks for a refund of 25 cents. Bad for her morale? A waste of time for which her company is paying her? Of course. But that's only part of the problem. Issuing trivial orders, and especially making improper requests, suggest that this executive has other, more critical shortcomings. Any executive who has his secretary chasing after his quarter may waste more time on trivia than he invests in important concerns.

The nation's secretaries are only too eager to reveal scores of commands they consider foolish, demeaning, and a detriment to efficiency. They have been ordered to empty piggy banks — those of the boss's children — and to roll the coins into packages; to scratch the boss's back daily at a prescribed hour; and even to clean his false teeth! And some have been caught between a boss's love affair and his wife.

Pettiness, small discourtesies, expense account liberties, and nepotism may be clues that a top manager feels superior to other people and is undermining the strengths that would otherwise make him effective. All managerial strategies may be indirectly confounded by the damage this person inflicts unknowingly on the organization. People want to respect the person at the top; they want to be proud of their organization. They will return pettiness for pettiness; dishonesty for dishonesty. Selfishness tears an organization apart.

Even when they think they are not being observed, managers' abuses have a way of impacting on other people's effectiveness or morale. At a company that was going through a financial squeeze, the word was passed to trim costs wherever possible. Two key managers continued their practice of taking each other to lunch and writing it off as a business expense. Naturally, they kept the fact secret. The company cashier knew what was going on, however. Their game cost them his respect, and who knows how much of a ripple effect this loss of respect had among other employees? Even without snitching, one person's lack of respect has a way of rubbing off on others.

Failure to respect people as beings who have ideas, feelings, and even the right answers can be costly. Take the case of the machinist who detected a design flaw in a set of plans from the engineering department. When he pointed it out to his supervisor, the supervisor chastised him for wasting time, told him that design wasn't any of his business, and ordered him back to work. Shortly after that, the worker's fears proved to be well founded. The flaw cost the company $50,000. That magnitude of unnecessary waste which workers observe first-hand, makes them wonder why management argues over a few cents per hour at the bargaining table.

On the giving end, a manager can make equally costly mistakes. The more information withheld from his or her people, the less chance of developing a working relationship with them. This form of manipulation results in less-than-maximum performance. Carried to the extreme, it can backfire, with disastrous results. When one machinery-building company decided to move to a new plant, some of its managers decided that telling the workers about the move in advance would only upset them and interfere with production. Another group of managers, including the communications department, had a billboard erected at the new site telling the whole story. Many employees passed the billboard on the way to work. On the afternoon of the first day the billboard was up, management denied all rumors of a move. Production plummeted and management credibility took a nosedive.

A manager's fear of dealing with people as people can manifest itself in attempts to evoke fear in others. One manager used to call meetings for 6:30 AM, and warn everyone to be there. Then he would call a meeting for 8:30 PM, issuing the same warning. After a while, his subordinates caught on to what he was doing. One by one, they left him high and dry. Managing through fear is rapidly losing its effectiveness with today's enlightened and economically independent workforce.

In the struggle for security, a manager can be trapped into overcontrolling people and situations, and get into trouble by setting too many rules. Some rule-making should be left to the people who have to live with the rules. At times, the manager is most effective when pointing out a problem and leaving the answer to those who know what constitutes a good, workable solution.

A manager whose plant was plagued by accidents vowed to do something about it. First, he initiated a detailed, time-consuming reporting procedure, which included entries for "cause" and "future prevention." Apparently, he needed to point out that accidents were running too high, but his solution did not produce meaningful results. Before long, reporting injuries became such a tiresome task that supervisors discouraged workers from going to the dispensary. Floor bosses began carrying aspirin and Band-Aids just to avoid filling out reports. The procedure produced mountains of information — mostly useless. One worker, for example, hit his thumbnail with a hammer. As the cause of mishap, he reported: "Hit wrong nail." Prevention: "Hit right nail."

This manager's next directive elevated the ridiculous situation to the absurd. Suspecting that safety standards weren't being enforced, he ordered supervisors to report a minimum number of safety violations each week. At first, workers took turns deliberately breaking the rules so supervisors could meet their quotas. Later, the supervisors tired of turning in their own people, so they began to wander around the plant, looking for someone else's workers to report. Despite all the reporting being done, no attempt was made to find the actual causes of accidents.

Workers inevitably fashion their own codes of conduct. The manager who has a positive view of people sets out problems, objectives, and aspirations before them so they will devise a code that serves both their interests and those of the company. The manager who tries to set all the rules is inviting defiance. People will see the imperfections in the system. They will fight to develop their own system — imperfect as it may be — to counter the one that is imposed on them.

UNWAVERING BUT WRONG

"The decision has been made and I'm not going to change it." All too often, managers commit themselves to a decision that has proven to be a bad one even before it's implemented. Sometimes the decision itself is good but improper decision-making procedures create problems along the way. Certain people may have been offended by not having their ideas heard or by being told of a change at an inopportune time. Again, the pretense of perfection gets in the way of sound management.

One high-ranking manager was determined not to correct a major organizational problem that called for centralizing an operation under his control. The reason? Several years earlier, he had been the manager down the line who had decentralized that operation. His original decision was right but things had changed. His big mistake was in being overly concerned with appearing consistent.

Successful managers like Robert Malott, chairman of FMC Corporation, are willing to change in response to changed conditions. He was the driving force, in 1972, behind the consolidation of four fragmented operating units into two functional groups. In 1978, however, he led a reversal — this time decentralizing the company into nine business groups. He believed the change would speed growth by "pushing down" operational responsibilities and requiring higher performance from streamlined middle and lower management.

The manager's adversary is always change. Either the manager will master change or will be mastered by it. The more perfect a manager is in maintaining the corporate routine, the less likely he or she is to make necessary changes. On the other hand, an impatient manager may hastily try to break routine and wind up causing a new brand of problems; intensity of purpose blinds him or her to some of the things going on — the emotional reactions of people. Newly assigned to an organization with a poor performance record, for example, a manager may be tempted to "clean house" immediately. A more experienced manager might tread more slowly at first, making friends, building loyalties, sensing out feelings, assimilating facts, and looking for explanations behind the routines.

THE NEWLY APPOINTED

The manager who assumes a new position — whether it's a first position or not — must accept the high odds of stumbling into mistakes or falling victim to some unexpected adventures. At some point, he or she may be overwhelmed by "the things they didn't tell me about the new job." Some events may bring painful reminders of personal imperfections.

Ron left the serenity and security of systems analysis, confident that his new managerial task of production control superintendent would bring him greater rewards, more satisfaction, and a brighter future. He soon found that he had bitten off a lethal dose of confusion and confidence-rocking self-doubt.

With the challenges and promises of a move into management, Mike walked briskly into the New York headquarters only to discover that he had neglected to make one rather vital arrangement — he had no office.

For Ron, the shift from systems analysis, where the pace was leisurely and allowed for careful planning, to managing the helter-skelter world of production work on a plant floor was shocking. "It was wild. Everything is NOW! You have to think on your feet; there is no time to fully analyze anything. Too often, you don't concentrate on one thing, you try to do a little of everything," he says, and adds, "I wasn't a total stranger to the department, either. I had worked with the men there for about seven years. But working with a department and becoming part of it are two different things." It took Ron about seven weeks to feel he was beginning to know his way around. After he got the learning experience under his belt, he was promoted out of it — back to systems as manager of systems and planning.

There are many reasons why the new job produces the unexpected. The executives who conduct the interviews and do the appointing may be derelict; they may fail to fully describe the duties to a newly appointed manager because they don't dare to or they don't care to. They may be afraid of scaring off the person they have selected to fill the spot. Or they may figure that he should learn the hard way, just as they did. It's possible, too, that they may simply not be aware of the problems the new manager will face.

The usual practice is to discuss only the basics of the job before a person is appointed. Not all the little troubles that are going to occur can be foreseen. As for the big problems that come up — that's what the new manager is being assigned to handle. Theoretically, at least, the individual's experience and potential have been matched with the scope of problems he or she is apt to encounter in the job. If all the major problems could be foreseen, there might be no need to assign a manager there.

Another good reason for letting the newly appointed manager discover problems for himself is that what one person regards as a problem is no problem at all for another. Individuals vary widely in what bothers them, what problems they are able to uncover, and how they handle trouble. A critical aspect of the hiring process, therefore, is the definition of the limits of the new manager's authority, so he or she will know what the boundaries are when tackling problems. Each manager will have a personal, unique approach to working within that framework.

The new manager may step into existing personality clashes. Some may not be flagged because they are not even recognized. Sometimes the new appointee's predecessor thinks of himself as the one with the personality problem, figuring that his departure will end the situation, or the appointing senior manager may assume that is the case. Unless the personality problem is a major one, it may be best not to call it to the attention of the newcomer, who then can enter the situation without bias, letting everyone start with a clean slate. If the problem persists, the new manager can size it up and deal with it then.

Entry into a new position elevates the normal tendency to put on a show of superiority. The newly appointed manager, whose ego is boosted by the recent promotion and yet threatened by the unknowns of the new assignment, may try too hard to display his or her strengths. "Don't give anyone the impression that you're the messiah arriving to save them," warns one vice president, who, time and again, has watched capable managers suffer misfortune simply because they tried to impress their co-workers.

People are more impressed by the ability to zoom in and ask questions that get to the heart of the matter. Managers who wave their intelligence or knowledge like banners are asking for trouble. A good manager doesn't necessarily know more about the situation than anyone else, but has the ability to uncover the factors that lead to a sound decision.

As a newly appointed manager, you can strengthen your position by learning all you can about your future supervisor (and company, if you are making that change), the products, company programs that will affect you, and the people with whom you will be dealing. Ideally, you should develop this information before you accept the job, but it's difficult to overcome the flattery of a job offer and thoroughly study the situation. The job may be totally different from what was portrayed by the people who recruited you. In one case, an engineer accepted a post as director of plastics research with a metals-oriented company. He accepted the job without visiting the company's facilities or meeting any of its people except those who first contacted him. His first exposure was a shock. The company had no plastics research operation; he was it! In addition, he learned that he was one of the first outsiders ever brought into the company in a position of responsibility. His arrival was bitterly resented, and, in less than two years, he left.

Studying the history of the position as soon as you arrive can help cut through some of your inevitable confusion and minimize the further confusion you might cause. A review of your predecessor's records and correspondence will provide some clues as to what he or she spent time on and serve as a base on which to build or to consider making deliberate changes. When you don't know the situation, your actions may represent a change of course without your realizing it. If you contemplate making changes, talk them over with the people concerned. Changes should not come as a surprise to the people affected by them.

Awareness of the situation also helps you set meaningful objectives. An overzealous manager may set inflexible deadlines to meet specific goals before settling into the job and being able to realistically determine what needs to be done and what the time factors will be. Knowing where the authority and capabilities lie in the organization is the key to what a person will be able to accomplish and how long it will take. That's why getting to know the people-resources is the number one priority for a new manager. Learning how people in the company relate to one another is a close second; company organization charts and job descriptions often do not tell the true story.

A new manager can turn to subordinates for some of the information needed, but should be well prepared to explain why it is needed and how it will help everybody concerned, advises one experienced manager. "Why?" is an increasingly popular question asked by workers today. They want to know the significance of what they are doing. Encountering a new manager, the question takes on special importance to them; they want to size up the new boss. They want to know if "the new guy" is asking the right questions, how he is approaching things, what he is interested in. They are trying to anticipate the way he is going to operate.

There can be some surprises hidden behind the answers a manager gets or doesn't get. Quite often, the early protestors and resisters turn into valuable employees, while those who quietly acquiesce may not be interested in the general welfare — instead, they are waiting for the new manager to make a major blunder.

A new position tests character as well as knowledge and skills. Because a manager is human, he or she becomes part of the problems and the solutions surrounding the job. That may be one of the unmentioned reasons for not writing detailed job descriptions for managers. Seldom accurate, job descriptions risk confining the powers of the truly effective person. Many companies prefer to let managers "write" their own job descriptions and revise them as they go.

Even with a full understanding of the situation into which he or she is stepping, the new manager may be hit hard by the emotional impact of living with the job. When, for example, Dick assumed the executive vice presidency, he knew he would be responsible for endless day-to-day decisions. Still aglow with the feelings that a major promotion can bring, he found himself forced to decide about a plant shutdown — suspend operations at one division, sending long-time employees out into the cold, or run deeply in the red. "It's not exactly a surprise, but you still don't recognize the weight of it all," he says.

"AM I AN 'US' OR A 'THEM'?"

People's allegiances form the vital cement that can bind together an organization or solidify it into small lumps that will not fuse with one another. But to whom does a manager owe allegiance? The bosses up the line or the people in the lower echelons? Periodically, a manager is haunted by that question.

When you're newly promoted into management, the question gnaws especially painfully. Your position has changed; you're more aware than ever that you are in the middle. If you now head a group of former colleagues, you ask yourself: "Am I still one of *us*? Do these people figure they can get away with anything now?

Do they think I've turned my back on them?" Increasingly, you find yourself in the position of implementing policy and making the kinds of decisions that you and the gang used to complain about. You miss that. You wonder how much they are grumbling about you now. You may be tempted to relive the old times and join the group, showing them you really still think management is all wet. Or you may be tempted to put on a mask of superiority and insist that they shut up and accept the system.

Don't expect the griping to stop. It will go on, but that doesn't mean you can't get the job done. It's when the griping stops that you should worry, experienced managers advise. That may indicate that your people are apathetic or so hostile that they won't speak. Griping and knocking company policies are standard procedures in most organizations. It's a problem only when it gets in the way of performance. What looks like resistance may be a normal form of feedback.

Some of the griping may be directed to you. "You're our representative to *them*," your people believe. They expect to be able to feed information upward through you. When things don't work out that way, they feel shut out of the organization. At the same time, upper management expects to hear what's going on "out there." If they have to rely on indirect pipelines, they aren't getting all they expect from you. They want you to pull an oar for your operation.

Successful managers take the position that you have to be both an *us* and a *them*. You not only have to be capable of passing reports to your superiors, you've got to make the people who work for you understand what the corporate goals and objectives are and why they have been set in a given way. That means a manager has to understand the scheme of things, and that's not always the case.

Some policies and procedures are easy to relate to your subordinates because they are fairly straightforward and obviously logical. Others are new, difficult to understand, or unpleasant to accept. You not only face the difficulty of "motivating" your workers; you may lack the necessary motivation yourself.

What do you do if you don't "buy" a decision made by upper management? Ignore it? Accept it blindly? Effective managers do neither. They take steps to sell themselves on it one way or another. That involves getting to top management and working to understand their reasoning, or, if necessary, helping them "improve" their decision. Few senior managers today expect to get away with a "just do it and don't ask questions" reaction to honest questioning.

If you shrink from challenging questionable objectives or assignments, you're not doing anyone a favor. If you go back to your employees acting like a helpless middleman, that's how they'll treat you. You won't get them to achieve the results expected by top management if they are stewing in discontent, evading or fighting your directions.

On the other hand, if you go to your people with a good explanation of what they are to do, you can expose the broader picture to them and help them see where they fit in. By explaining the significance of their assignment, you can help them find satisfaction in a definite job against which you and they can measure their performance.

Naturally, you won't always get the full explanation from upper management. Maybe there just isn't time. Then you operate on trust. Occasionally, you will have to relay an order which you don't understand, but if you and your bosses have had a good batting average, chances are your people will say, "We don't like it, but he's convinced, so that's good enough."

When you follow instructions responsibly, you have a better chance of getting responsible performance down the line. The better managers demonstrate that being effective means being a loyal leader of your people and a loyal follower of upper management.

When the gears grind, the manager in the middle serves as the lubricant. It can be bruising. Both sides constantly remind you that things have to be improved. The trick is to see yourself as a positive ingredient, not as a sacrificial offering. You have to show that you are interested in something other than your own skin. It has been said many times that a manager has to win the respect of the workers — not engage in popularity contests. Serving as the lubricant between *us* and *them* is the best way to do it.

Respect is not enough for some managers. They prefer comradeship. But management is a lonely game. Interests, problems, status, income, and many other things change with each increase in responsibility, threatening to increase the distance between you and others. Outside the job, too, friends may either not be changing or may be changing in different ways. Old friendships may wither. Ironically, the more people a manager manages, the greater the distances become. The manager runs the risk of feeling he or she isn't an *us* with anyone.

7
Who Will Make the Decisions?

Powerful as he was, Alexander the Great had a scheme for delegating authority and building allegiances. He commanded his generals to marry the daughters of conquered princes. That way, the generals' management goals were likely to be in line with the needs of the countries they were to rule, as well as with Alexander's wishes. At the same time, the subjects were being ruled by their own royalty. Unfortunately, many managers measure their success in terms of the power and authority they can keep to themselves. In the traditional hierarchy, tight controls restrict decision-making powers to a few powerful persons.

Scientific management has been allowing, in recent years, for greater dispersal of decision-making authority. "Learn to delegate responsibilities," many a manager has heard. Yet the urging ran counter to measures of stature and effectiveness. All the emotions fired by the realities of the workplace fought against anything that appeared to be a surrendering of your responsibilities.

Today, the thrust toward decentralized decision-making has intensified. Companies are finding that they can make more effective decisions by inviting inputs from a greater number of participants and by pushing the responsibility for decisions down to the lowest possible level of management, even letting non-managers make certain decisions. The autocrat is no longer as effective nor as honored as he once was.

THE PUSH FOR PARTICIPATION

The movement to participative management seems irreversible since it is propelled by a number of diverse forces. It responds to the needs of the organizations, the people in them, and the people served by them. Most of the direct force has been coming from enlightened managers up to now. Faced with the need to improve productivity, they realize that not all gains will or can come from investment in plant and equipment. They are convinced that new approaches to work and organization will enable people to produce better results. They are not quite sure what the optimum approach is, but they are experimenting with ways to restructure jobs and people relationships to put untapped talent to use.

Advocates of participative management recognize that involving more people in the decision-making process can improve the quality of decisions and enhance the chances of successful implementation. "It's only sensible to ask the person who does the work — who knows the work — for ideas on how best to do the work!" says William M. Ellinghaus, president of American Telephone and Telegraph Company. "Or as one of our employees told us: 'Involve me in decisions that involve me!' "

"Over the past ten years there has been a remarkable increase in employee expectations for participation in decisions that affect their jobs,"says Jerome Rosow, president, Work in America Institute. "This desire is specific to the immediate arena of the job and work-related issues," Mr. Rosow points out. "It does not reach up to executive decisions or corporate-wide decisions which extend beyond the individual employee's ken or beyond his limited vision of the organization."

Participative management has caught on in Europe, but in a different fashion and for different reasons. There, it is politically and ideologically based, coming in response to demands for letting workers share in the management, if not the ownership, of their companies. Codetermination — the concept of placing representatives of the workers on either the board of directors or on the management board — has little support even among labor leaders in the U.S.

While "participation" or "industrial democracy" has been institutionalized in Europe, there is still a wide gap between worker and manager on a day-to-day basis. In the U.S., there is far more give-and-take in daily operations, and U.S. workers are better informed about their companies. The approaches employed here vary from one company to another as pragmatic responses to a range of needs on the parts of both the worker and the particular company. Their dollars-and-cents value is mixed with humanistic and democratic motivations, extending people's freedom into the workplace. If participative management were only an ideological catch-phrase, it might soon lose momentum, but it is a broad and deep change, cutting its way into our changing society.

Because they owe so much of their existence to adversarial relations, labor union leaders are dragging their heels on participative management. Some workers have been slow to accept it because it demands greater responsibility and involvement. A significant percentage of the workforce does not want to be involved in making decisions – so they say. They have been taught to expect only the hygienic rewards from work. Some managers, however, see through the demands for higher pay and more time off. They believe workers have an underlying desire for more freedom, greater respect as individuals, recognition, and work that is more psychologically rewarding.

Some resistance comes from managers, too, since participative management threatens their prerogatives – their ability to control other people. Some have neither the confidence nor the patience to allow others to take some control over their own work. There are also institutionalized deterrents to participative management. In situations where decisions and procedures are set at a centralized point, there is little latitude for an individual manager or work-group to make a significant contribution even insofar as modifying their own tasks. As new facilities are built or new organizations formed, however, management is increasingly likely to embrace some form of participative management rather than an orthodox hierarchy.

Non-managers as well as managers are more educated and more independent than – and have higher expectations than did – their predecessors. The powerful needs of individuals and organizations make a welcome match that, in the years ahead, will permit workers to share in decision-making and to commit more of themselves to the execution of those decisions. In this groundswell of change are the seeds of the corporation of tomorrow. The drive toward humanagement promises to elevate the quality of decision-making, improve the organization's sensitivity to the world outside in its goal-setting, and raise people's level of commitment to those corporate goals.

Participative management is working in companies that operate according to humanistic values. Others that try to superimpose it on managers who don't embrace those values fail because they are trying to use it as a device simply for improving productivity — seeking the by-product. At least as yet, no single program or set of techniques seems to be universally acceptable. Companies experimenting with participative management insist on being flexible in their approaches, permitting local units to devise their own techniques tailored to their own needs and capabilities.

Participative management or democratization of the workplace has to be built on a coming together of worker and management. It is the product of a cooperative rather than an adversary relationship. The Japanese have long been admired for their impressive productivity improvements and the quality of their products. They have amazed American managers even more by exporting their philosophy to the U.S., where they have established manufacturing facilities in recent years. Their style allows for a "bottom up" decision-making process rather than the usual American process of "top down" order-giving. Managers of Japanese-owned plants in the U.S. advise that, in order to achieve the results of the Japanese style of management, you must:

- Work to build confidence in your workers.
- Replace boss-subordinate relationships with equal-to-equal ones.
- End the practice of making the stockholder happy in favor of making a vital resource happy: the worker.
- Move to consensus decision-making.

Decision-making in Japanese management systems both here and at home involve top executives and hourly workers. "Every employee feels that he or she can effect change, and this prevents them from feeling isolated from the top," explains William Nelson, vice president of Kikkoman Foods, Inc. There is also a humanistic linking of manufacturers, suppliers, and customers, called the "cycle of goodness." This concept rules out unreasonable attitudes and fosters a strong working relationship that produces a "warm feeling." The Japanese firms seem to be succeeding with such concepts even in this relatively adversarial culture.

HOW YOU GET RESULTS MAKES A DIFFERENCE

Until the last decade or so, management style wasn't a matter of serious concern. Companies were generally structured in such a way that managers had to be activity-oriented, keeping an operation going any way they could. In more recent times, the trend switched to results-orientation as companies struggled to maximize the effectiveness of those operations. Now, with the social revolution of the last decade or two, management style has taken on new importance. Management is caught between its results-orientation and the demand for people-orientation coming from the public, from workers, and from managers themselves.

The tasks or goals of the corporation are becoming increasingly people-related as pressures for social responsibility, applied internally as well as externally, change the results a company may seek and the means it uses to go after them. Management is learning that getting results is not all that counts; people are concerned with *how* you get them. A manager has to find the time and energy to show as much concern for the way his or her people are working as for what they are doing. Management experts point out that managers now have to understand group processes. But they also have to understand individuals — each person's wants, needs, aspirations, capabilities, and limitations.

In the 1960's, Douglas McGregor — famous for his "theory x" and "theory y" — asserted that management should change their assumptions about people. The traditional view — theory x — was based on the assumption that people are passive, lazy, and reluctant to accept responsibility. He did not deny that some people fit this description, but claimed that this model did not reflect human nature. It was, rather, the result of centuries of experience in organizations that treated people according to that assumption. Advancing a new approach to managing people, McGregor suggested that managers should be responsible for helping them realize their potential for work and responsibility — theory y.

A manipulative manager is not concerned with drawing upon a worker's full potential. He or she divides the work into tasks and gets people to work within these limitations, thus setting up a win/lose situation. But people are no longer willing to be on the losing end; therefore, a manager has to struggle to find win/win relationships.

In today's management styles, "in" is out. There is less and less room for insensitivity, insincerity, and intimidation. The manager who is overly results-oriented under-utilizes the people who work for him or her, and may rob the organization by pre-setting limitations on people's performance and by crushing interpersonal relationships that are needed to attain corporate goals. The effective styles today are founded on a positive view of people and the ability to instill positive attitudes in others.

Obviously, not all managers are people-oriented. Some see tasks and activities as their prime concern and view people as something to be overcome or manipulated into getting the job done. There is still room for such managers, depending on the industry, the company, or the job function. But the sweep of change among workers and fellow managers will slowly whittle away at their effectiveness and acceptance. They will not be the managers who apply great leverage to the organizations of the future.

As the authoritative style of management is eroded, business will need people who can lead without commanding, who can find power in common purpose rather than depending on the trappings of hierarchy. A manager who can see himself more as a collaborator than as a conqueror can capitalize on people's insistence that they be given more meaningful work and a voice in decisions that directly affect their work. Negotiating consensus among thinking, working people will not make the manager's job any easier, but it will tend to make him more effective. Done well, it can eliminate the problems of worker boredom, absenteeism, grievances, strikes, and declining productivity.

Dispersal of decision-making authority isn't a cure-all for problems of productivity, morale, or motivation, warns psychologist and motivation authority Frederick Herzberg. If a worker doesn't like a job to begin with, the pressures applied by fellow workers in a participative situation will increase the discontent. If he or she takes part in the decision-making process and is constantly over-ridden, unhappiness increases. Herzberg believes, too, that permitting a group to participate in its own management might develop good interpersonal relations, but that it might also become a power base for counterproductive actions. When group autonomy becomes the goal of the new structure, individuals may be short-changed as much as in an authoritative organization. Far more must be done than injecting some decision-making opportunities into the daily routine. Management has to stand back and redesign the job structure and interpersonal climate in its organization.

The trend to a more humanistic style of management does not mean that all managers will operate alike. There are as many styles as there are managers. Even among the most successful, there are countless variations. There are firefighters and opportunists, impulsive managers and deliberative ones. There are active people who take the initiative, and reactive ones who are good at responding to problems when they present themselves. There are high-riskers and cautious types.

Every manager has a style, whether he is aware of it or not. This style casts an image of himself and the organization. The image seen by superiors, subordinates, peers, and outsiders will determine, to a great extent, how they'll interact with him. Elementary as it may seem, you should want others to see you in a way that permits you to be effective. Superiors want managers who can help them accomplish their objectives. Subordinates want a leader who helps them and welcomes their assistance. Fellow managers want to associate with someone who is knowledgeable in his field and who can help them.

WHAT'S THE BEST STYLE?

A number of things determine which management style works best. One of the prime determinants, of course, is the manager.

A manager's personality, knowledge, needs, and goals suit him or her for certain styles. To a large degree, style is determined by where a manager thinks the expertise lies — within himself or within others. A manager will either want to drive people with specific instructions or will unleash them in a way that brings their talents to bear on the situation.

The expectations of the people who work for the manager also have a bearing on which management style is effective. Some workers want to discuss everything before they act; others expect to be told what to do. Some have valuable inputs and important questions; others don't think enough about the operation to be effective participants in decision-making.

The nature of your position or department also determines how much you can involve others in decision-making and how much time and talent are available for collaboration. If you're in charge of long-range planning, the bulk of your work is fact-finding, judgment gathering, and discussion. On the other hand, if you're in charge of shipping, the basic job is to move those goods. This does not mean, however, that there are some jobs that permit no collaboration. Even routine operations, where no discussion is needed in carrying out the work, can be periodically discussed by the people involved in order to draw out ideas for improvement. You and your employees do not need to vote on which goods are to be moved, but two-way communication might improve both the process and people's attitudes toward their work.

Regardless of the style you find appropriate for most days, there is always the chance that a special condition will arise and force you to switch to another style. An emergency is an obvious reason for a temporary change; you may not have time to be collaborative. In a normally hectic operation, you may occasionally discover a break when you can stand aside with your people and catch up on some needed discussion. Or the political situation in the company may change and force you to raise or lower your profile for a short time. The better managers use a "mixed bag" of styles to fit the situation. But varying your style from day to day or mood to mood can cause trouble. If you're a hard-nosed manager by instinct and generally follow that style, don't confound your people by playing "Mr. Loveable" for an hour or two now and then. If you're a collaborative leader and generally involve your people in decision-making, don't explode into fits of dictatorship. Sensible flexibility in style is valuable, but crossing that fine line into inconsistency can cost you dearly in people's trust.

Depending on the type of manager you are in your early years, you may have to undergo some changes in style over the years. A brash young manager can be effective, for example. But brashness is seldom effective and sometimes ridiculous for a 50-year-old. As a salesman or project engineer, you can succeed as a firefighter, jumping into crises and operating independently, but when you move up the line to broader responsibilities, you may have to become more reflective, future-oriented, and collaborative.

A vice president of manufacturing confesses that he has evolved into quite a different manager than he was early in his career. "In my early development, I used principally the dictatorial method. But I quickly learned that the extra time invested with others in the organization, learning their ideas, materially improved the quality of the decision and very substantially increased the effectiveness of implementation. I also learned that most of these people really know their business, have valuable contributions to make, and can become more involved, committed, and productive." This manager didn't evolve naturally or easily. As a do-it-yourselfer, he caused a lot of grumbling, but feedback from his supervisors sensitized him to this defect. He did something about it. He read management theory and studied management techniques. At one point in his career, he even hired an industrial psychologist to work with him and his staff a couple of days a month to critique their style of work.

The management styles prevailing in the company and — particularly — the styles of your boss play an important part in determining which style you will use. In mature companies, customs and expectations tend to dampen styles which don't fit the company pattern. Newer, fast-growing companies are generally more flexible; they allow wide variation in style and high degrees of risk-taking. Where top management does set a pattern, it is not always deliberately attempting to mold every manager into a common shape. Their example is often contagious. Since it works, people copy it. A carbon copy of upper management is not always what the company needs, however. You may succeed by complementing upper management rather than duplicating it — provided you're compatible.

Extremely different management styles can sometimes be seen in one company over a relatively short period of time. First, a chief executive runs the company as a one-man show. He and the company are reasonably successful. He does not take the time to develop a strong management team and makes no serious effort to prepare a successor. Then the chief executive resigns or retires. There is no obvious successor to fill his shoes. If there is, he hasn't been prepared for the responsibilities of the job. Suffering either from the lack of authority or preparation or both, the new chief executive turns to a radically different management style from that of his predecessor. He manages by committee. A management group provides coordinated input for decisions, and it makes the decisions. It does not always select the right course of action, but it does offer one important advantage: no one person can be blamed for failure or mediocre performance. Neither the one-man show nor the committee approach can lift a company to maximum effectiveness. Both lack an important ingredient for that: leadership.

LEADERSHIP: A SPECIAL QUALITY

Great works are done by great people. Great works can also be done by ordinary people when they follow great leaders. The workload of our institutions far exceeds the available supply of great leaders, so we entrust it largely to managers. Unfortunately, the terms "leader" and "manager" are often used interchangeably. But they are different.

A leader has a strong sense of personal identity and purpose. Leaders will take high risks in order to achieve what they believe in. Included in this is the willingness to open themselves to others, sharing their ideas, and learning from others in order to find common purpose. To a leader, the organization is a device to help (and, it is to be hoped, not to hinder) people in their attainment of goals.

A manager may or may not be strong in leadership qualities. He or she may simply accept and support whatever purpose has been set for the organization. Managers are likely to link their survival to the survival of the organization — or whatever portion of the organization they are responsible for.

A leader doesn't necessarily do all the things that many organizations expect of a manager. For the leader, the goal comes first; the organization is secondary. Owners, employees, and others may prefer to entrust the organization to someone who, above all else, will see to its survival, its permanence. In this sense, organizations are often designed with a bias against leaders. In strict hierarchical organization, leadership qualities among non-management employees are viewed as a threat to the system. But with the rise of individualism on the part of managers and non-managers, autocratic rule is giving way to leadership — wherever it can be found. As humanagement extends democracy into the workplace, it looks for leaders to develop consensus amidst what would otherwise be chaos.

DEGREES OF PARTICIPATION

Even in a democratic, humanistic setting, decision-making is essentially a dictatorial act. Although you may invite participation and input from subordinates before decisions are made, it's your role to weigh the facts and opinions, lend your own experience and judgment, and commit to what you determined to be the best course. As one company president explains: "My subordinates have got to leap in and curb things, direct the efforts of my decision-making. However, when all the votes are in, so to speak, or when everybody has had an opportunity to voice his opinion, I'm the one who has still got to make the decision."

There are degrees to which you may choose to involve subordinates in decision-making. You can explain a decision which you have made and ask a subordinate to consider the best way to implement it, present possible solutions and let him or her evaluate them and make the decision, or lay out the problem and let the subordinate suggest solutions. Or you can totally delegate a particular area of responsibility, letting a subordinate anticipate the problems and arrive at his or her own solutions.

The degree to which you let subordinates participate depends on a number of factors: how critical a risk is involved, how much input your people can furnish in the way of information and meaningful opinions, and how much emotional content has to be "aired."

Effective managers can sense when an upcoming decision involves heavy emotional content. They know that these factors can make or break the implementation of such decisions and possibly have long-lasting effects on people's performance. By involving others in the decision-making process, a manager stands a better chance of learning the feelings of subordinates and their evaluation of how others will be affected — other departments, customers, stockholders, etc.

The earlier you include subordinates in discussing proposed action, the better the chances of their understanding why a particular course is chosen and becoming interested in its success. If they have an objection to the end or the means, you had better know about it before the implementation is underway. This is the time to bring them around to your way of thinking or to change your mind if they bring up points you have overlooked.

Delegating decision-making responsibility to others develops their abilities and frees you to take up more general responsibilities. If you are genuinely convinced that your subordinates lack the necessary information and experience for a task you are going to delegate, you can guide them to the information and opinions they need. If there isn't sufficient time for research, you can help them directly — short of making the decision yourself. Managers too often take the easy way out, forcing their subordinates to miss the opportunity to acquire new knowledge and the experience of managing their way through new territory.

There are situations in any organization where pressures and high stakes seem to call for a senior executive to step in and direct things with an experienced hand. Even then, he or she must try to avoid playing dictator. To cover most situations, it's best to establish procedures for reviewing decisions and changing course before running so close to disaster that the senior manager has to step in. This permits subordinates to manage but lets the senior manager maintain close communication and control. There is no reason for anyone to assume that once you delegate authority you never intend to be heard from again. If you do step in, it's important to call people together as soon as possible and explain why you did things the way you did.

Regardless of who is making a decision — you or a subordinate — a good review and monitoring system will improve both managerial effectiveness and the learning process. You and your subordinates can play "Monday morning quarterback" constructively, analyzing why a particular decision worked well or failed or how it could have been improved.

Grabbing the reins occasionally won't be disruptive if you have an established record of letting your people run the show most of the time. They can accept the fact that you have to assume ultimate responsibility on special occasions. One senior manager says that when he has to reverse someone's decision, he sometimes makes a friendly bet about who turns out to be right. When he's wrong, he admits it and takes corrective action. People can accept an honest mistake. Analyzing what unforeseen circumstances made the decision wrong will help you as well as your subordinates learn. People will respect a learner far more than a know-it-all.

For those managers who are convinced that they know so much and subordinates so little, it is a wrenching experience to delegate decision-making authority. It is much easier to hold the reins yourself unless you are a leader who wants to involve others in doing a job together. As you move up the management ladder, you face the pressing need to free yourself of minor responsibilities and petty tasks. With each rung, the tasks you shed are more significant. In time, they become fairly major. As you embrace a wider range of activities, you have no choice but to delegate. The questions are: what do you delegate, how, how much, and to whom?

THE ART OF CUTTING LOOSE

Some managers think they are delegating when they are simply tossing off trivial chores "I have my secretary open my mail," one will say. "I give the computational work to someone else to do," another says, sighing with relief. "A girl brings my coffee whenever I want it," yet another boasts. You can work a secretary or other subordinates hard and yet not delegate any responsibility for decision-making.

Genuine delegation includes such things as:

- Problems which require exploration, study, and recommendations for decisions.

- Any activity which you feel is within, or even slightly beyond, the scope of a subordinate's job and abilities.

- Any task which taps talent in a positive way, especially one which promotes company goals or the individual's development.

- Any activity which, if well handled by the subordinate, would save you time and expand his or her outlook.

The work that you regard as dull might be interesting to someone else, but you have to walk that fine line between suggesting that you are dumping some detail work on them and overselling the tasks as the world's biggest assignment. Whether you are concerned about moving up or intent on doing a better job where you are, delegate work to people to the extent of their abilities. Delegation is the fine art of determining each person's capabilities. That's why it takes time. That's why so many managers are poor at it.

A manager needs to maintain control yet has to set goals with wide parameters, leaving as much room as possible for subordinates to exercise initiative and discretion. That means preparing people to accept responsibility — not just throwing work at them. Managers who fail to lay solid foundations and delegate work to people who aren't ready to handle the assigned responsibilities create bad situations. The failures that result convince them that they never should have delegated the responsibility in the first place and that they should never do it again.

One successful delegator devises "mini-business capsules" for his people. He gives them some authority for hiring and firing, some money, and some facilities to manage. He promises to let them know when they're off course. He spends extra time with a person who is experiencing difficulty and, when necessary, he has temporarily withdrawn people, telling them "this thing is bigger than you at the moment; you need some help and I'm going to give it to you." When someone falls short of meeting a goal and the reason doesn't appear to be incompetence, he tries to avoid reacting emotionally and usually asks, "Where did *I* go wrong?" The most common answer is that he failed to communicate adequately what was expected or what solutions are not tolerable.

To be a manager who delegates successfully:

- Welcome the ideas of others. You may also be able to implant an idea in the minds of others and later compliment them for having originated it.

- Accept mistakes as part of the investment in people development.

- Severely limit your criticism of failure.

- Rarely tell your people *how* to do something.

It's easier to delegate if you see the managerial role as that of a catalyst — to stimulate action without being consumed. The higher you rise in the organization, the more important this catalytic role becomes. Early in your career, you do things yourself and get fairly immediate feedback on the results. As you move up in responsibility, you have to tell someone else to do that work so you can cover all the essentials of your job. That requires thinking creatively and creating thinking subordinates. Managers who set goals that are too broad or too difficult to attain without help are more likely to delegate responsibilities to others. They are committed to a goal and have no desire to take refuge in details.

The manager of managers, in turn, has to watch that subordinates don't try to do all the work directly rather than serving as catalysts. One way to get them to operate as they should is to give them more work than they can handle alone and then treat them as catalysts. The manager cannot urge them to avoid getting lost in details and then proceed to question them about the fine points of their operation.

8
Changing Organizations

Schoolbooks say: the stockholders own the corporation and delegate their power and authority through the board of directors to the chief executive, who, in turn, delegates certain powers to others; everyone owes his or her power to someone up the line. In truth, the flow of power and accountability is not that neat. Power does not emanate solely from the stockholder. It doesn't always flow downward.

Novels and movies suggest that corporate power is a crown for the people who politick best. Power originates inside the corporation, it is said, and the principal activity of managers is to wrestle with one another for the power. Actually, though people rival for position and influence in any organization, the corporate world is not inherently a jungle.

Management hopes that organizations are models of efficiency and effectiveness, that power is exercised in an orderly manner. Systems compensate for human weaknesses, in other words. But, in reality, organizations also nurture and compound human weaknesses. They may try to control or compensate for them, structuring relationships in which people check on one another to weed out the inevitable mistakes and compete with one another to heighten performance.

None of the usual notions about corporate power offer a sound basis for understanding the present — much less the future — corporate situation. Whatever grains of truth they may contain will be lost in the swirl of change blowing through the corporation.

When stockholders and top management are no longer in complete control and have to yield to government, labor, and special interest groups, the corporation as we know it loses purpose and power. As people demand the opportunity to engage in meaningful work and personal relationships, the hierarchical power structure short circuits. Corporate power is beginning to emanate from different sources.

NEW SOURCES OF AUTHORITY

Corporate power is far more dispersed than ever before, and this trend will continue. Until recent years, it was primarily economically based and closely guarded. In the past, the owner of the company could do essentially what he wanted. He did the hiring and firing as he saw fit. He selected the organization's objectives. As companies grew in size, some of the power had to be delegated to others. People sometimes vied for control of these slices of power – either through ownership or through seizure of one of the positions to which power had been delegated. Possession of power was generally the authority to use it.

Power is the ability to do something. Authority is the right to use that power, and in this era of "rights," authority does not originate entirely within the ownership or management of an organization. Management increasingly has to seek its authority from those whom it manages and for whom it manages (not only stockholders, but customers and the public). There is a growing interdependency of people within organizations and between the corporation and the rest of the world.

The chief executive of a company may look powerful. But one of the CEO's primary functions today is to tend to the sources of power originating outside the corporation – beyond the stockholders. Throughout the 1960's and 1970's, corporate management has heard again and again that business exists only so long as it performs the functions set out for it by society. Much of what is happening in today's corporation is dictated by outside forces other than the marketplace. Investment plans are heavily influenced by the need to control pollution. Hiring practices have to fit the laws and regulations regarding equal opportunity for women and minorities. Product design and pricing policies are dictated by regulators, legislators, and public interest groups, in a quest for durability, reliability, and safety.

People complain today that institutions are not responsive to them. Corporations, they say, are becoming too large and too inhumane. Ironically, they are levying their demands on the corporation in more ways than ever before. They are also more protected from corporate abuse than at any time in the history of the corporation. While the corporation has attained great financial and technical power, it is losing the power to act freely. While workers and the public perceive management as being powerful, management feels increasingly powerless.

Pressures from the outside have created some new deposits of power inside the corporation. For many years, people have joked about the chief executive who refuses to make a major move without first consulting his attorneys. Now an executive may also first have to consult environmental experts, public relations experts, technology experts, personnel experts, *and* attorneys. Other people's authority of expertise can stop the chief executive in his or her tracks. The power that once went automatically with certain positions is being challenged by a better educated, more demanding workforce — bluecollar, whitecollar, professional, and managerial. The power of knowledge and the power of persuasion are becoming the driving force in business as never before.

Members of a rigidly structured institution must be willing to accept authority as given and direct their loyalty to the organization. This mortar for the corporate pyramid is crumbling, however. People now attach their allegiances to themselves and their families, to their profession, and to other organizations. Yet, most corporations are hierarchical in structure, modeled after the ancient religious and military institutions. They have a top and a bottom. The top tries to tell the bottom what to do through layers of middle.

The orthodox hierarchy is designed to handle a relatively constant situation in terms of its membership and its tasks. But now we see people come and go in the corporation; individuals change in the way they work or in what they want to do, sometimes changing careers. We see corporations dealing with new lines of business, managing lines that are in various stages of maturity, and concerned with issues that are not related strictly to the company's products.

The organizational limits we have put on ourselves frequently prevent us from being fully effective in attaining the organization's objectives as well as in realizing our personal goals, but the "profession" of management was born in hierarchy to master these limitations. So now we find our organizations over-managed, under-led, and under-achieving. Time and time again, managers have estimated that they are only about 50 percent effective. Reasonable estimates suggest that the average company is 25 percent overstaffed in its management ranks.

Overstaffing is sometimes the result of not tailoring the work to what's really happening. Some of the work that managers do isn't necessary. Under-utilization of their talent can be blamed on either individual managers' lack of motivation or the organization's failure to make use of their skills and energy. Too many organizational limits on what a manager can do dulls creativity and discourages him from growing beyond the bounds of a specific job — one which might appropriately have a limited life span anyway. A company sometimes creates "management" positions to support individuals whom it is reluctant to fire; if the company has made mistakes in promoting people, it may promote them further, assigning them to "harmless" functions — or nonfunctions.

POLITICS: THE POWER TO DO OR UNDO

Organizational limits and overstaffing complicate any cooperative effort. They raise the political content of the organization. Politics exist in all organizations from the multibillion dollar corporation to the smalltown church or the P.T.A. because politics essentially is the process of doing things with or through people. People are in quest of what they think is best for them. How they go about achieving this is politics. Some managers see it as a means of getting things done *with* people. A minority may resort to sneakiness, foul play, lying, cheating, and any other devious means of getting things done *despite* people.

Unfortunately, organizational politics usually bears the bad connotation — not the creation of power to work with people but the abuse of power to undo people. Corporate life does not seethe with politicking and bad relationships, however. Two-thirds of the managers surveyed on several occasions over the years by *Industry Week* indicate that their relations with both their peers and their supervisors are good; the rest rate them as satisfactory.

Whatever the ratio of good to bad politics in your organization, you cannot ignore them and still do a good job. Your ability to perform well depends on working with other people. There's no such thing as staying out of politics. You can only hope to turn politics into good human relations — an essential part of the managerial role.

If your subordinates engage in politicking (destructive politics), there are several ways to fight it: stressing performance and letting it be known that it's the only way to survive in present positions or to get ahead; defining jobs carefully so that subordinates know what is expected of them and how they are elevated, so they can perform without undue confusion and conflict; and short-circuiting those who are devious and getting rid of the unethical ones.

Occasionally, managers find that they are involved in a political situation with their boss. The dynamic subordinate manager who poses a threat from the boss's point of view may become the target of undermining. The better the subordinate's performance, the more threatening the manager appears and the more the boss retaliates with such tactics as selling him short to senior management. If this manager has to go around the boss to get things done, he may become an easy target for the boss who wants to cry "Politics!" (Not all the knife-wielding in corporate politics is done against the boss or peers!)

A political struggle in the echelons above you is hard to ignore since your future may be at stake. If two managers are slugging it out for the top position of your division or company, you have to make some tough decisions. Both of them may become extremely cautious, afraid to make commitments for fear they'll make a mistake that will give the other an opening. Or they may abandon long-term considerations and take drastic action to produce good short-term results. If they are putting their personal goals above those of the company, where do you place your allegiance? Most managers believe you owe it to the company rather than to either of the struggling top managers in a case such as this.

When a group of managers was asked what they would do in this situation, most felt they couldn't do much. But they would probably try to get through to these battling superiors. The first step would be to collect information to document fears about the company's future. After analyzing the facts and confirming that there is a problem, they would next follow the organization's line of reporting and make their fears known. If possible, they'd get other managers to join with them and file joint reports. And they would make it a series of reports rather than a single report. The reports, including suggested plans to remedy problems, would go to both warring managers with a request for approval on corrective action.

If you follow this procedure, be ready for some flak, they warn. Make sure your own house is in order so it can withstand scrutiny in case anyone comes down to find out what this troublemaker is up to. You, and others who have joined with you, have to stand ready to prove you are an island of competency in the midst of a highly political situation.

If the reports get you nowhere, some managers suggest leaking them to the level of management above the power struggle. But be prepared for the consequences if things don't work out, they say. Be ready to look for a new job. A few managers say they would, at this point, align themselves with one of the warring managers. This, too, is a high-risk tactic. It's advised especially in cases where one of the managers is more competent than the other but lacks the confidence to win the battle; support and documentation may provide the boost needed for success.

Understanding company politics is a matter of comprehending the informal organization within the formal organization, identifying the people who make decisions and those who influence them. It requires seeing the real world behind the organizational charts and official statements. You can't keep up with the realities of an organization simply by reading the reports and memos and attending staff meetings. You have to plug into the informal communications. Call it tapping the grapevine, maintaining an early warning system, or listening to the rumor mill.

The smart manager collects and integrates the hard information of formal communications and the vibrations felt along the grapevine.

Although it may not be accurate in the rumors it conveys, the grapevine can give you clues to what people perceive to be true and what they want to be true. Understanding people's perceptions and wants is vital if you are going to work with them. The rumblings you pick up from workers can give you an early warning of things to come. When you're tuned in, you don't have to wait until feelings erupt into demands from union leaders. And the signals you get from top management can help you anticipate change rather than waiting until it is formalized and pushed on you.

The best way to tap the grapevine is to feed it — to give in order to receive. But you have to stick to open and honest discussions of what you perceive is going on and stay away from gossip for the sake of discussion. Access to the grapevine is not based on treachery; a good link-up depends on honesty and mutual trust. That doesn't mean the grapevine should carry only good news. Quite to the contrary, it often carries information about conflict. But since conflict is such a vital ingredient to corporate life, it pays to be able to tune in.

BUILT-IN CAUSES OF CONFLICT

In addition to the differences of personality, style, background, and viewpoint that a manager has to contend with, some conflict is built into organizations. Policies, rules, and structure are established to suppress conflict, but they do not eliminate it. And they are the cause of some of it. The specialization of functions, the design of reward systems, and the controls and checks imposed on members of an organization can put otherwise cooperative people at odds with one another.

Specialization leads people to stake out territories and practice departmentalized thinking. The company is working for goals that should be common throughout, but each department has its assigned index for success. This often sets departments at cross-purposes with one another. The sales manager who depends on a large part of his or her income from meeting sales forecasts plays it safe and forecasts conservatively. Then he or she works hard to exceed that forecast. On the other side of the departmental wall, the manufacturing manager is usually paid according to his ability to produce within budget and fill orders on time, and manufacturing plans are based on the sales manager's conservative forecast. Then, when sales run higher than that false target, the manufacturing manager has to assign workers overtime and make other costly adjustments, falling behind schedule and shattering the departmental budget.

An organization's rewards system may encourage this waste, creating internal rivalries and undermining long-range objectives, particularly if the organization is geared to the short-term. The manager who has an easy time in a boom year might get a good bonus. The struggling manager who is doing a good job holding a difficult operation together in tough times and building for the future may get little or no bonus.

The parochial view influences a high percentage of management decisions. In fact, some companies are merely collections of parochial views; they have little direction other than the drift that results from people's pursuing their individual courses of action. People overlook the fact that if anyone in the company has a problem, everyone in the company has a problem. The manager who realizes this looks for mutual benefits in his or her dealings with other departments. Such managers don't force their way in by asking, "What's going on here?" They take the time to learn about other departments' goals, their problems, how they can help. And they anticipate how other departments can help them. You're more likely to get cooperation when people think you can and will help them meet their goals. Other people are also more likely to serve long-term goals if they know where the organization wants to go and how they can contribute.

Some structural design is intended to produce a controlled conflict. Much of the accounting function, for example, is aimed at controlling the spending of other departments. A quality control section is generally set up to be a policing agency, catching mistakes of the production department (not that this is necessarily the best way to maximize product quality). A department charged with controlling someone else's costs or quality tends to look most successful when it interferes most with the performance of another department. Financial controls are sometimes stacked in tiers that don't "add up" to the people who have to operate with them. A department may labor to come up with a budget for the year; as it works within this budget — monitoring its own progress — Accounting or Purchasing may say, "You can't spend this; you can't buy that." Delays and disputes cost untold dollars as the operating unit fights to exercise what it regards as its rights under the budget it has already won.

Corporate cost-cutters have had a relatively free rein in recent years — especially in newly merged organizations, where management has looked for quick turnarounds and profit improvement. Some routine activities and expenses are wasteful; sharp-pencil managers can make savings that will not hurt corporate effectiveness. Sometimes, however, someone may try to look good by cutting vital expenditures or by delaying them. The impact on the operating unit's effectiveness and on its morale cost the company far more than the eager cost-cutters are aware — or, sometimes, care.

Sometimes a manager will structure a competition between candidates for promotion, hoping to force them to peak performance. They and others may expend a great deal of energy but not necessarily toward achieving corporate goals. In the scrap for individual power, the tempo of the organization looks fast, but the company may only be spinning its wheels, doing too few of the right things for the long term.

CORPORATE FLEXIBILITY

Effectiveness is not only a matter of doing things right but of doing the right things. This is a time when people are changing their definition of corporate effectiveness. As their needs and wants change, so does the nature of their organizations.

"One mark of every great organization is its willingness to change — to adapt to new needs and to new opportunities," said Frank T. Cary, chairman of International Business Machines Corp., when the company made a number of significant changes in its organizational structure in 1974. For most of man's history, however, the mark of a great organization has been its ability to resist change. Today, corporate structures have to be revised to meet political, economic, environmental, and competitive demands.

In the 1950's, and particularly during the "go-go" 1960's, the decentralized structure was popular. Power or authority in such areas as capital spending was delegated to division managers or group executives. Many companies embarked on massive expansion and diversification programs. Their entrepreneurial approach fitted well with the behavioral theory that autonomy fosters greater motivation and achievement among managers.

The 1970's, a period when the need for tighter controls at the top was felt due to tight money and regulatory uncertainties, brought a gradual shift by many companies to a more centralized structure. The shortage of qualified managers also contributed to the move toward centralization, which generally requires fewer managers — particularly entrepreneurial types — and makes greater use of specialists.

Whether a company leans toward centralization or decentralization does not, in itself, indicate a greater or lesser adaptability to change. At either extreme, there are creative, flexible, growing, and changing organizations and others that stress constancy and preservation of the organization as their primary objective.

Some organizations, or parts of them, pulse with people who are enthusiastic and have a sense of urgency. Others get the job done when they get around to it. Poor tempo can result from the structure itself or the people within it. It can be fostered by a lack of clarity about who is responsible for making a particular decision, by a lack of deadlines, or by a lack of determination as to who is to execute a decision. Despite a high level of activity, little gets done. People who are working hard may not be doing the right things. Long hours and laborious decision-making processes may reflect an organization that has a slow tempo.

Some organizations function effectively only because certain managers ignore the structure. They go around channels to get the information they need or to forward information to people who have the authority to act on it. Over the long term, the extra effort expended by these managers may result in confusion for others who are forced to sort out what *is* from what is supposed to be. The procedures and relationships that are getting things done don't match those spelled out in policy statements and organization charts.

For obvious reasons, you can get into trouble by skipping anyone in the chain of command above you in a hierarchical organization. You can also cause trouble by skipping downward, bypassing subordinate managers. When you deal directly with lower echelon managers or workers, you may place them in an untenable position by putting them at cross-purposes with their immediate superiors; in their effort to please you, they do something their boss knows nothing about or with which he or she would disagree. Or they might elect to ignore any agreements with you, hoping you'll forget them as they return to what their supervisor expects them to be doing.

When the boss has to step into a subordinate's area of responsibility and deal with a particular situation directly, he should first explain that this is a special case and that responsibility is being assumed only temporarily. Stepping in without a careful explanation raises the subordinate's doubts about the boss's confidence in him. Done too often, it suggests that either the subordinate is not performing as expected or that the boss is out of line.

Many managers feel it is a good idea to skip down through the ranks occasionally and talk directly with workers. It's a good way to stay in tune with things if you operate through the structure, getting the cooperation of the subordinate managers in between. If, however, the bypassing is more than talk — if it becomes a new working relationship stemming from a lack of confidence in the subordinate manager — it's time for a discussion of performance or for a change in people.

Some managers enjoy demonstrating their dynamism, directness, and decisiveness by stepping into situations and making promises or laying down decisions. The managers in the middle whom they bypass don't have an opportunity to furnish facts and opinions that would influence the top manager's decision; they learn too late that "things have been changed." They may find that their people have been asked to do something that pulls them away from their regular duties. There are times when the subordinate may initially welcome the commitment made by the top manager, then later discover that budgetary or other established limitations prevent him from carrying out the special agreement. The subordinate has been given a driver's license — but no key to the car. When managers depart from the norm in hierarchical or autocratic structures, they may cause more perplexity than progress — more conflict than cooperation.

SEARCHING FOR WIN/WIN SOLUTIONS

Management has traditionally been at home with competition — both in terms of pitting one's company against another and in terms of individual advancement. Today, however, a few top executives are beginning to talk about the need for cooperation — externally and intracompany. They recognize that competition is a win/lose proposition. A major challenge to tomorrow's corporation, they suspect, will be to find win/win solutions to the many problems besetting it. That calls for a style of conduct beyond the experience of most people — humanagement — to permit everyone to feel he or she has truly won, or, at least, not surrendered something of himself. The design and operation of organizations based on cooperation depends on humanagement's basically optimistic view of the nature of mankind. Humanagement can save American business from the divisiveness that has torn other industrialized nations' economies by heading off unreasonable demands from employees, attacks by a disgruntled public, and invasion by regulators — none of which solve the basic problem of conflict.

People become more aggressive and less cooperative when the means for satisfying their wants become limited. In the 1980's and 1990's, the large bulge in the population entering the age range for top professional and middle management jobs could create a destructively competitive climate. Unless people have learned to manage through cooperation by then, we may find our corporations boiling with hostility. If organizations continue to open up, ease their structural rigidity, and forget about putting people into boxes on an organization chart, the population bulge will approach the corporation as a wealth of talent anxious to put itself to work, rather than as bodies competing for a limited number of predesignated positions.

A growing number of companies hire talented people and let them define their own jobs to a large degree. One young manager recently described the loose structure in which he is working: "I'm not exactly sure who my 'boss' is. If three particular people walked into my office and told me to do different things, I'd probably just sit there in neutral." He does well and enjoys this situation where smooth operation depends on cooperation and flexibility rather than on a rigid chain of command.

For some people, such a situation would be threatening. Along with greater independence, they would have to accept greater interdependence. The price of working in a flexible organization is the willingness to be flexible, and many people aren't ready to pay that price — to abandon the old structures (regardless of how much they dislike them).

Yet, their reluctance as individuals doesn't match the implications of what they demand collectively. Society is losing patience with the surrender of freedom at work and undue conflict and ambiguity in organizations. People seem to leave themselves little choice, then, but to accept the responsibility that goes hand in hand with freedom. Rigid structures prevent them from attaining the self-fulfillment they want as individuals and from meeting their expectations of one another. Their search for a sense of community and self-identity puts them in direct opposition to the formal structures to which they are accustomed.

Humanagement offers a way out of this dilemma, to unify individual wants and corporate needs, and to find a workable middle ground between hierarchy and no structure at all. It can enable people to break out of limited relationships, which encourage selfishness and conflict, by their treating one another as whole persons. Thus there would be less need to jealously trade minimum investment of themselves for the maximum selfish gain. Showing respect for the individual and leading the way to corporate commitment, humanagement can replace mechanisms which reduce people to something less than people and prevent organizations from being equal to the sum of their parts.

9
Treating Workers as People

In late 1977, when Carborundum Company received a tender offer from Eaton Corporation, top management knew that the door had been opened for a takeover by someone. William Wendel, then Carborundum's president, says his chief objective from that point was "taking care of the people" − getting the best possible price for the shareholders and preserving jobs, salaries, and employee fringe benefits. Later, when Carborundum was on the auction block, as several firms bid for control, Mr. Wendel − in the privacy of his hotel room in New York City − jotted down some of the things that were running through his mind. Chief among them were concern that the company's stock was rising in the market and that "the people who built the company were restricted from trading while speculators profited greatly."

Some people might be surprised that the man who had spent 16 years at the helm of a company, building it to $600 million in annual sales, would lose any sleep out of concern for his people. Others who know Bill Wendel would insist that the company's success was due to his interest in the welfare and the talents of his people.

Managers tend to hesitate showing consideration for workers for fear they will be taken advantage of. The new thinking in management, however, is that, with proper treatment, people will take advantage of the opportunities to learn, grow, and fulfill themselves. Both the employer and the employee will benefit in a win/win relationship.

Once, a manager was master and the subordinates were clearly subordinate in every way. People have traditionally surrendered their freedom and individualism at the plant gate. A person's self-denial won him economic reward. But today people tend to be less willing to deny themselves. They do not want to be faceless parts of faceless organizations. They are concerned about the content of their work and what it means to them, and they are concerned about the impact of the fruits of their work. They don't want to create harmful products or despoil the environment. They are turning to their organizations for self-fulfillment, not self-denial.

"Living within a free and open democratic political system, the American worker expects conditions within the workplace to be compatible with political and social conditions in other aspects of life," says Jerome Rosow, president of the Work in America Institute. "These expectations include the right to free speech, the right to privacy, the right to dissent, the right to fair and equitable treatment, and the right to due process in all work-related activities."

There is more to people's rising expectations than less work for more pay. Although some are happy when their job doesn't involve much work, many are dissatisfied with organizations that stand in their way of doing a good job at meaningful work. While unemployment is a major concern in this country, far more people are suffering from *under*employment.

"Attitude surveys of youth have revealed consistently that the work ethic is strong and alive, despite the revolution in social values," says Rosow. "However, youth's appraisal of the traditional rewards of hard work has certainly changed. In 1967, a 69 percent majority answered 'yes' to the question: 'Does hard work always pay off?' By 1975, 75 percent of American students answered this question '*no*.' This view of the world of work is probably a reflection of attitudes expressed at home and may also be a realistic insight that many jobs are routine, dull and boring, and do not challenge the talents of the average better educated worker." Research by the Louis Harris Associates opinion research firm shows that more than eight out of ten workers welcome challenges to their creative abilities. More than seven out of ten say they want to be involved in efforts where people cooperate rather than compete.

Florence Skelly, executive vice president of Yankelovich, Skelly and White, Inc., lists what she considers to be the work values of the under-35 group that influence attitudes of much of today's workforce:

1. Concern for meaningful work.
2. Shift of energy and attention to leisure time activities.
3. Renewed focus on money in order to find fulfilling leisure time.
4. Super-confidence and rejection of authority, plus fear because they know they have gotten away with less rigorous standards.
5. Indifference to traditional penalties for poor performance because internal feelings of inadequacy or pointlessness are often more painful than being fired.
6. Intense need for feedback on how they are doing – of being accepted as individuals.
7. Stepped-up sense of time – living for today – and maybe readiness to take on more at an earlier age.
8. Receptivity to excitement, novelty, change, and adventure at work.
9. Wide array of lifestyles and needs – more pluralistic, less conformist.

What the manager has, therefore, is a workforce ready to challenge and to be challenged. The "problem" of higher expectations carries with it its own solution – a solution that is problematical to the manager who insists on clinging to old views and managing in the old style. He or she must respond to what people want from their work and capitalize on what they can contribute. Accepting the old assumptions, the manager can say, "People don't want to work today." And this negative view of people will be self-reinforcing. When a manager discounts the positive contributions people can make and struggles to avoid failure, sure enough – people respond negatively. Acting upon the humanistic assumption and unleashing people's drive for success, the manager finds that they are capable of testing his ability to stay ahead of them.

A WORKFORCE OF INDIVIDUALS

Obviously, not all workers are alike in their attitudes. Some have been turned off by work as they know it and will do little more than collect compensation for their time. But the majority will do a good job and are looking for the opportunity to do far more. Thanks to their education and mobility, they *can* do more. When they don't find fulfillment in their work, they demand more time off to pursue it or at least to escape boredom.

Americans see themselves in highly individualistic terms today. "While they appreciate that they are part of a larger organization, they feel strongly that they and their jobs deserve individual attention," says William Ellinghaus, president of AT&T. "As one of our people commented recently: 'We have a million people in the Bell System and I don't want to be treated like a millionth of anything.'"

Individualism does not pose a threat to those who genuinely believe that management's role is one of managing change. "Innovation and flexibility are the prime institutional requirements of management," observes James H. Jordan, vice president of employee relations for ICI Americas, Inc. "Management philosophy is predicated on the theory of individual merit and progress of the individual. Thus its institutional framework is consistent and coincides with the new forces impacting on the workforce."

Dr. Jordan suggests that the trend toward individualism and humanistic management runs counter to the interests of organized labor and will meet opposition there. "Unions are built on a foundation of group control and their behavior is predicated on a notion of group action which contradicts and appears to violate the central tenets of individualism."

These tenets also run counter to the management practice of regarding workers as "overhead" — something to be minimized and controlled. Now, with the tables turned, workers may regard the manager as overhead unless they see that he or she is helping them to do their job. That's why managers increasingly see their role as helping people understand what needs to be done, why, and how they can help. They feel responsible for providing the resources and information people need and for finding ways to help them develop their talents. Their concern for workers' well-being equals their interest in improving productivity.

The broadening use of humanistic forms of management is not a capitulation simply to keep peace. Successful applications permit people to give more of themselves as they derive more from their work. This new approach complicates the managerial role and demands more attention to workers as individuals. Managers now work toward making labor more effective rather than simply cutting labor costs. They strive to maximize what individuals can do rather than confining them to some predetermined tasks. They know that if people give you only what you ask for or command, you're getting only a fraction of what they're capable of giving. People can beat any incentive program; they can figure out better ways of getting the job done. "So why not take advantage of what they have to offer?" some managers are asking.

THE QUALITY OF WORKLIFE

At General Motors, management has imposed on itself the support of a program called "Quality of Worklife." Its roots date back to 1969, when outside research indicated that performance and job satisfaction could be improved through cooperation, involvement, and personal growth. But what could be done in a corporate giant, where many of the jobs were highly mechanized and routine? In 1971, every general manager of every division was invited to a conference to report on anything he might be doing toward these ends. At that time, these efforts were optional. Today, they are not. The form they take is determined by local management and union officials in each operating unit, however.

The Quality of Worklife program is "not a happiness program, not an incentive program, not an effort to make work fun, easy, and undisciplined; but to make it effective, challenging, and involving," says Stephen H. Fuller, vice president of personnel administration and development. It aims toward more employee involvement on the factory floor and in the office, better cooperation between union and management, better design of jobs and organizations, and the integration of people and technology.

Some General Motors plants are now employing work teams which operate without supervision. Workers select new employees to be on the team and are responsible for training, forecasting material needs and scrap rates, and planning their work. Some plants have established assessment centers in which hourly workers evaluate job applicants.

The company's Tarrytown, N.Y. assembly plant was a serious problem plant a decade ago. Torn by hostility, costs were running high and performance was poor. In 1977, management and the union initiated a three-day training program on problem-solving. All 3600 employees attended on a voluntary basis over the next year and a half. The $1.4 million investment has paid off in high morale, low absenteeism, a reduction of grievances, and improved quality of worklife and product. Today, the Tarrytown plant is one of the best in the GM network.

WORKERS "READ" THE BOSS

Success for the manager and the organization boil down to treating people properly. While people may vary in attitude toward work, they all harbor a basic desire to be respected as individuals. Their happiness and effectiveness, therefore, depend in a large part on one-on-one relations with their manager. The "boss" is a major influence on people's effectiveness. Their development into better workers or managers depends largely on him or her. They judge their jobs and their company largely in terms of whether they feel they have a good boss or a bad one.

Industry Week surveys show that managers think they are relating well with their subordinates. Three out of four say their relations down the line are "good." On the other hand, as they look up the corporate ladder, they are slightly less enthusiastic; about two out of three call those relationships "good."

Managers may work at building good relations with workers in their formal dealings and written communications, but unsuspectingly cause problems through their nonverbal communications. They sometimes fail to see the relationship between their actions and how people interpret them. A vice president of industrial relations cites the case in which a company caught two foremen stealing. The foremen were punished by demotion to the hourly ranks. This may have been a fairly natural response on the part of management. "But what does this tell hourly workers about what you think of them?" this vice president asks. Mistakes like this are common, reflecting a misunderstanding of people and their emotions.

The manager's behavior and people's interpretation of it emotionally charge the workplace. If he or she seems to withhold information, fails to invite an individual to a meeting, shows up unexpectedly, or even looks at an individual in certain ways, people will wonder why. Rightly or wrongly, they will find significance in the boss's behavior. Without knowing it, he or she may be breeding suspicion, fear, and disloyalty. Each subordinate may interpret a certain action differently, too. Seeing the door to the boss's office closed, for example, one subordinate may feel cut off, while another might say, "Great! I can do my own thing!" Without feedback, subordinates can misread you and stumble into countless unnecessary problems. One of the worst kinds of managers is the one who says: "If you don't hear from me, you'll know you're doing a good job." Managers who do that aren't doing their jobs.

Psychologists tell us that people consciously or unconsciously look for security, belonging, influence, and self-esteem in their work. Much of the elaborate mechanism of supervision, control, and discipline is a carryover from times when workers really were not part of the organization and had little choice but to accept insignificant jobs and to function as appendages to machines or processes.

Dr. Frederick Herzberg lists several factors that can contribute to a person's finding motivation within the job itself: direct and quick feedback on performance, new learning as part of the job, development of unique expertise, control of the resources used in the job, authority to communicate with others — particularly in a client relationship with others whose work relates directly to his, the opportunity to schedule his own work, and personal accountability for that work. Sharing information on a two-way basis is imperative for working effectively and building a sense of belonging. People can gain a sense of influence when they share in decisions about matters that concern them directly. Their self-esteem grows as they see themselves shaping the situation in which they work.

The autocratic manager tells workers very little. Therefore, he can often get away with knowing less. In a more open setting, the manager has to fully understand his own operations, be more aware of what is going on in the entire organization, and convey as much of this to the workers as possible. Managers who work with knowledge workers — people who are essentially handling information — find this even more important. These people are especially demanding of information, not only to perform in the immediate job, but because they tend to be learners and want to continually expand their understanding of where they fit in.

THE END OF ISOLATION

When a manager was a man who was isolated from his people, operating without showing emotion or regard for the emotions of others, and keeping most of the decision-making burden to himself, his work was simpler and clearer than it is for a manager operating in the more demanding humanagement atmosphere. Neatness and clarity have a place in accounting or in solving an engineering problem, but not in managing people. Human relationships are seldom neat and rarely are predictable. To be successful in today's terms, a manager must be sure that he or she builds each individual's sense of personal worth and importance. Productivity depends increasingly on providing an environment in which the worker's motivation can be put into gear. Rather than saying, "Here is your work, do it," a manager is more likely to approach a worker and ask, "What do you need in order to do your job?"

The manager of the past endured the discomforts of isolation; the manager of the future will master the difficulties of sharing responsibility with others. Humanagement calls for reversing the tactics of the autocratic manager who felt it was important to admit no mistakes, to take credit for all the good ideas, to keep his or her plans and goals a secret, to talk down to subordinates, and to keep subordinates on the defensive. The mantle of perfection will no longer serve a useful purpose. Managers do make mistakes and workers know it. Sometimes workers are aware of mistakes even when the manager isn't, because they can see things falling short of what they know should be or could be. If the boss isn't interested in their advice, they'll find amusement in watching the "infallible" manager fail. On the other hand, they regard some things as mistakes because they see them from a limited viewpoint. Managers who keep too much to themselves increase the odds that people will think they see mistakes when there aren't any.

Discontent sometimes arises from the fact that rank and file workers often think a manager knows more than he or she really does. They assume the boss has all the answers — that there is a policy for everything, that every problem has been anticipated and a solution slated for it. When a manager permits people to see the risks being taken and the unknowns being wrestled with, they can find their work exciting rather than routine. When you encourage people to find ways to minimize the risk, their involvement and contribution climb dramatically.

It's difficult — and sometimes disastrous — to try to fake a participative style of management. You have to value people's inputs and yet be demanding of their output. People can sense when your solicitation of their ideas isn't genuine. And, of course, they can be turned off if they see that their inputs are not really having an impact on your decisions.

Solicitation of people's inputs has to be continuous — not sporadic — in order to foster participation. The manager who operates primarily as an autocrat and then occasionally asks for suggestions or reports on problems — perhaps even going so far as having "idea contests" — may force some inputs from some people. The manager who constantly deals openly and fairly, shares his or her hopes, and occasionally prods and frequently compliments the workers, is more likely to develop a good flow of change and improvement.

When communications are not taking place spontaneously, it's up to the manager to encourage dialogue. Many workers are not assertive, and a manager has to ease them into communicating by speaking positively to them and directly asking for their ideas — not on corporate strategy but on problems at their level, where they probably have useful information and definitely have feelings. The subordinate has to be given enough time to express himself so the boss can make a valid appraisal of the suggestions. If the boss then has to reject the idea, he has listened well enough to make a reasonable rebuttal.

Experienced managers seem to be divided on whether to be blunt when rejecting an idea. There's no substitute for frankness, some say. Other managers work up to a rejection gradually, since they find most people respond better to gentler treatment; they may start off acknowledging the good points and then proceed to the points of disagreement. Another trick some use: they ask the individual to put the idea in writing. Either the worker will not bother to follow it up or will find that the idea doesn't hold up well when it has to be expressed in writing. This is not simply a tactic for discouraging ideas; it may force the person to consider that new idea more carefully, refining it into something more valuable than its initial form. It reflects an atmosphere in which both boss and subordinate can learn.

Learning depends on "being able to disagree with the boss — even to be wrong — without his or her losing respect for you," says a plant manager. It also implies that the subordinate be willing to disagree. "People are sometimes afraid of the boss; I have to encourage them to argue with me," he adds. When a mistake or difference of opinion draws heavy negative criticism, many people will retreat. From then on, they are apt to play it safe. If the individual is not one of those who will independently learn from his or her mistakes, it's up to the boss to direct the subordinate's thoughts to what went wrong and why.

A good subordinate constantly seeks coaching and feedback on his performance. If the boss shirks coaching responsibilities, a dynamic subordinate will eventually conclude that he can develop only by resigning and looking elsewhere for coaching. Often, the subordinate's needs coincide with the boss's goals and are easy to satisfy. An effective manager has to find special assignments and educational opportunities for this dynamic subordinate, or even arrange a transfer. Independence and drive are not signs of disloyalty, but a worker may move elsewhere if the boss isn't willing to collaborate.

THE AUTHORITY TO INFLUENCE OTHERS

Some managers might regard all this sharing and caring as undermining their authority. But the vital authority in the corporation is not something that is bestowed upon you — one of the trappings of position. Today, you earn your authority with knowledge and abilities that permit you to help others put their power to work.

Better educated workers — managers included — resent authoritarianism, "but they are not opposed to proper exercise of authority," points out Jerome Rosow of the Work in America Institute. "This distinction is quite important. They respect authority properly exercised with restraint and with rationality, but reject authority which is abusive or arbitrary. This poses a challenge for large bureaucratic organizations to rationalize their work procedures and learn the art of managing conflict with consent."

There are few organizations that will select their key managers on the basis of something other than competence. The demands on them are too great to be dealt with by people relying strictly on formal authority. The person who develops new skills, takes on new problems, and offers fresh solutions earns authority among his or her peers, subordinates, and top management. Such a person does not have to echo the common complaint: "If they want me to get the job done, they've got to give me more authority." (Surveys by *Industry Week* show that one-fourth of these managers lament that their authority is inadequate. They are not admitting they haven't developed enough authority; they are complaining that authority hasn't been given to them.) While an organization may set down definitions of what you cannot do, it's up to you to explore the limitations. The greater your competence and self-made authority, the more you will push the limits farther and farther away. Effective managers work with other people and departments and find that they are invited to expand their range of operations. They break free of the bonds that organizations tend to foster.

Ability to get things done depends on whether people pay attention to you. Unfortunately, too few managers spend enough time building influential relationships with their workers. If their contact is too brief or if they are distracted while they "listen," they aren't building influence. They join those who complain about not having the authority to wield more rewards or punishments. They can push for improved productivity, campaign for cost-consiousness, or fight for a better safety record, but unless they are in touch with people "on the shop floor," they won't wield much influence. They're not taking advantage of worker know-how and the vantage point they have for spotting problems — and solutions. By not sharing their hopes and plans, these managers allow little opportunity for developing a team that operates at maximum effectiveness.

Some executives work down past one, two, or three levels of middle managers to talk frequently and informally with workers in the shop or office. The chief executives of 20,000-employee companies obviously can't be in touch with everyone, but they can use the same approach with the several levels of managers directly below. People want assurance that management is interested in their part of the effort and is working just as hard as they are. They want to know what is going on in the total organization and they want to know that their ideas are being considered in decisions about their part of the operation.

If the manager knew everything the workers know, he or she would be the near-perfect manager. When managers fail to tap subordinates' knowledge of things in specific work areas, they are apt to make unnecessary mistakes and miss good opportunities for improvement. One company found that gleaning wisdom from the shop floor enabled it to avert some long-term problems and costs. It learned that before installing a new piece of equipment, it was a good idea to paint an outline on the floor at the chosen location because workers often supplied reasons why it wouldn't work well there — reasons overlooked by the engineers. It also found that the operators of a proposed piece of equipment could furnish good advice on designing it for ease of operation and maintenance. And one group of workers showed that the contemplated purchase of a $30,000 crane was unnecessary.

GROOMING AND DOOMING OTHERS

As people move up, one of their greater responsibilities becomes the development of the managers reporting to them. More and more top executives are looking closely at the records of managers for developing subordinates. Many insist that each manager develop candidates for his or her own job, making it a condition for promotion. Chairmen and presidents of major firms formally groom a successor several years prior to their retirement.

Grooming successors — going beyond mere selection — has traditionally not been pushed hard by companies. Managers were allowed to focus on short-term goals or their own personal career development. And the survival instinct works against taking an interest in the development of subordinates; it has been safer to assert that the worthy managers will emerge on their own.

"I don't have time for handholding. Besides, I don't want my best people promoted out from under me." That line of reasoning not only hurts the organization over the long term, it can result in the manager's own lack of mobility. Being indispensable where you are can be a curse if you want to move on to something else. "Our chief accountant is a brilliant guy," says the general manager of a division in a large corporation. "He should be handling a job with wider responsibilities at the corporate level, but I can't recommend him for promotion because we have no one to replace him. I suppose we'll have to go outside to find someone."

One of the greatest dangers of selecting subordinates for promotion is the tendency to look for "the guy like me." It's natural to want to select someone who has a similar background and who thinks like you. It's also easy to be fooled by articulate people whose verbal ability exceeds their ability to deliver results. But old school ties, family connections, and a stereotyped dress and behavior are less likely to play a part in a person's advancement than they once did. Performance is the overriding criterion, and companies have moved swiftly toward objective development and promotion practices. Grooming subordinates for promotion is not something that's done only on special occasions. It takes constant evaluation of performance, strengths, and weaknesses. You have to determine an individual's skills and needs and provide opportunity for exposure to others in the organization.

Some managers pick a pair of candidates, suggest to them that they have a shot at a promotion, and let them fight it out. They figure the best will rise to the top. For some reason, they assume "the best" will rise only if they are placed in competition. Under these conditions, however, the candidates are tempted to politick for the promotion and let their current jobs suffer. Often, the person who politicks best will win the promotion. Sometimes the animosity generated by this device — and the possible resultant division of employee loyalties down the line — will drive a good candidate to thinking that what will do himself and the organization the most good would be to leave the company.

Individuals should be made to feel that they have a good future with the organization, but no promises about specific promotions should be made too early in the game, experts advise. People may figure out their chances, and good coaching can help them make realistic estimates so they will not tend to aim too high or too low. The person being groomed for the boss's job may sense being in line for a promotion, and others may sense this, too. It is less likely to become a problem if the candidate is not made a "crown prince." Management has to make it clear that the door is open to all and that advancement depends upon performance. A track record of having made good selections in the past also helps. Unfortunately, surveys show that a large percentage of managers do not think highly of their organization's batting average in selecting good people for promotion.

In top management positions, the grooming for promotion is often more obvious. The person who has been selected as heir may move in with the incumbent. He or she meets with the same people, contributes information and opinions, and slowly takes on more responsibility and independence. Both the "heir" and the incumbent try to spot and treat any areas in which the heir lacks exposure or information.

After a candidate has been selected for promotion, particularly at the upper levels, management will generally hold discussions with those who were not selected. On the surface, they may solicit views on company progress and policies; behind it all, they seek to determine whether these individuals will work with the new leader, request a transfer, or leave the company. The procedure may be held essentially as a ritual for some persons, but in the case of "strong second" candidates, management is fearful of losing them and anxious to find what's needed to prevent recent events from injuring their effectiveness. These discussions can be tough on any senior manager. And when you think they are all over, there's always the possibility that someone you haven't thought about will come to your office and demand to know, "Why wasn't I picked for that job?"

Managers can make serious mistakes, with the best of intentions, when they give performance feedback to average or below-average subordinates. Too many undeserved pats on the back or too little constructive criticism can lead to inflated self-appraisals and expectations. People may construct inaccurate images of themselves, overestimating their strengths and misinterpreting the requirements for promotion.

A subordinate's promotion is not only a significant event in his life, but an occasion on which the manager puts his managerial judgment and authority on the line. Is this the right person? Is he or she ready now? Has a better qualified person been overlooked? How will the new manager's peers and subordinates react?

Firing a subordinate is even more critical. The boss shares in the trauma of an individual's loss of income, disruption of routine, family tension, and public humiliation. If the firing is due to weakness in character or performance, rather than budgetary necessity, the specific reasons should be documented. Stealing from the cash register or chasing secretaries are good reasons, but they're not common. Incompetence is a good reason, but it's hard to define.

When the point is reached where a person clearly has to be fired, a few things can be done to minimize the pain to all concerned. Management should work out a fair severance arrangement and get the person off the premises as soon as his job responsibilities can be transferred to someone else. Keeping the person around until he finds a new job creates a period for festering relations, experience has shown. Playing a waiting game, pressuring the individual into positions where there is no choice but to lose face and resign, is highly unfair to all concerned. He should be informed directly and factually of the termination and be given specific reasons. Honesty and fairness is the best a manager can bring to bear on the delicate job of managing people.

DISCIPLINE AS POSITIVE FORCE

When an employee breaks the rules, violates a trust, or otherwise behaves objectionably, you might like to say, "You're fired," and end the problem. After all, many managers still say, "People need discipline." Then you think about grievance procedures, arbitration precedents, posting of rules, the employee's record, and providing due process. And you recall that hasty, emotional, or unfair disciplinary actions can cause wildcat strikes, walkouts, sitdowns, or shutdowns.

Disciplinary action can start more problems than it solves unless managers understand the purpose of it and stay within certain procedural guidelines. Discipline accomplishes little when it is an end in itself; it can be beneficial when used as an instrument for improving productivity and human relations. Rather than presenting a learning situation for the employee, improper disciplining may teach the manager some painful lessons if other workers, the labor union, or arbitrators are brought into the confrontation.

An effective disciplinary system has to be consistent, fair, progressive, and corrective. It is far more sophisticated than many managers expect — or would like. They overlook many little violations, thereby encouraging repeat performances, and then come down hard when they finally explode in anger. One manager may give a written warning for an offense, while another will fire a violater for the same offense. The rules of today's workplace will not tolerate such inconsistencies. Because employees watch carefully to see that you treat people equally and fairly, a poor disciplinary system will undermine your authority. "There isn't a boss in the world who'll survive a concerted effort of his people to get rid of him," warns a forest products company president. Good disciplinary techniques will help you earn the respect you need if you are going to survive and be effective. Many a good manager has heard his people say: "You're an S.O.B., but you're fair." They take that as high praise.

A corrective system lets employees know what proper conduct is, helps the individual offender correct improper behavior, and warns others what will happen if they break the rules. This means you discipline progressively, not erratically. When you fire someone for incompetence, for example, you have to show that work standards are established, that the employee was told of his or her failure to meet them, that you provided adequate opportunity to improve performance, and that disciplinary action was applied progressively — not in one crackdown.

Penalties for repeated offenses should be progressively severe. For example, the first case of an individual's absenteeism can be treated with an oral warning. Later may come the use of a written warning, a short suspension, a longer suspension, and then a discharge. Offenses vary in the number of steps that are advisable. There are few, however, that merit one-step firing. The reason for progressive steps is to make discipline corrective — not punitive. If an employee can correct his conduct problem, you save turnover costs and earn respect as an effective manager, plus some self-respect and satisfaction from helping someone else become effective.

Because managers want to avoid conflict with their workers, they sometimes dance around problems and yield their right to demand performance. When the offender's peers see no corrective action being taken, they lose respect for management. The manager who was looking for the easy route now has to turn around an entire work group – not just one person.

This unwillingness to be candid about problem employees has prompted many companies to push harder on their annual performance appraisals. Although these meetings provide an opportunity for managers to discuss problems with individuals, they are not a cure-all. Annual or semi-annual reviews by no means coincide with the occurrence of specific problems. Matters of discipline have to be dealt with quickly. This does not mean a manager should rush in and verbally bombard the violater. It pays to check with the worker's peers, former supervisors, and the employee relations department. If that doesn't reveal a possible cause and solution, a chat with the worker might throw light on the underlying problem. Often, say successful managers, the supervisor needs to listen and look rather than talk.

WHEN PERSONAL PROBLEMS CAUSE PERFORMANCE PROBLEMS

Your secretary comes in an hour late most days. Your right-hand man is cheating on his wife. Your lead foreman constantly bends your ear about his financial troubles. One of your best workers has gone sour – something is bothering him, but he won't talk.

Should a manager be concerned with his or her employee's personal problems? If so, to what degree? Should the boss play psychiatrist? Substitute parent? Bosom buddy? There is precedent for the entire range of involvement by managers plagued by this common problem. The sensible approach seems to be to draw a line between those problems that are work-related and those that are not. The individual should be judged on the basis of performance and any discussion of personal matters should be confined to their impact on performance.

When personal problems spill over into working hours as absenteeism, tardiness, fatigue, grouchiness, or hostility, the individual should have a chance to explain the poor performance. He needs to know that the boss is looking at what's happening in business terms and that what has been agreed upon as the worker's contribution is not being delivered. If the subordinate isn't confronted, he may assume it doesn't matter how well the work is being done and that may compound the original worries. The boss shouldn't plunge in with: "Tell me your personal problems." He has to convey the idea that it is understood that a personal problem may be the cause of the work-related problem, and that he is willing to listen to it.

A person may not be aware of causing trouble for others. Friendly confrontation exposes the situation, and suggests that corrective action is necessary. It's a start toward getting the worker to contain the problem and perhaps to solve it. If a worker does open up and begin discussing a personal problem, the manager has to be sympathetic and give that person a reasonable amount of time for finding a solution. A manager might be able to steer a subordinate to someone who has gone through a similar situation, or to an expert if professional help is needed. This is the danger point at which managers are sometimes tempted to cross the line and play advisor or problem-solver. A few really do help; they are especially good at counseling or have some experience in the particular matter at hand. Unfortunately, they are outnumbered by those who have crossed that line and made things worse.

The boss's knowledge of an employee's personal life can both help and hurt. The adverse things he or she knows about an employee can bias the boss's view of the worker in the work environment. On the other hand, they may help the manager see the employee in a more favorable light, since not all personal problems are dark and ugly. Maybe it's just that the subordinate's golf game has slumped! The more you know the employee in terms of interests and outside abilities, the better you may be able to make meaningful work assignments or promotions. But this can lead to the old problem of favoritism. "Objectivity" has been the watchword in the treatment of employees. But it may not always lead to getting the most from − or giving the most to − people. It's possible to be objective as well as personal if performance is the basic guideline.

OPERATING IN A PERSONAL MANNER

Managers who advise against treading into the personal affairs of workers don't suggest that you be calloused, inconsiderate, or aloof.

They place great importance on operating in a "personal manner." They judge other managers on their ability to get out and talk with workers, asking appropriate questions of anyone, including the janitor.

One successful executive has found the personal approach accomplishes two important things. "First, you give the person the human dignity he really deserves. After all, he's out there trying to make money for your company. You ought to talk to him and get his input. That does something for him, but − second − it does something for you. It gives you a pulse of the operation which you cannot get from any computer printout." Some managers say they have developed an understanding of people's inner feelings by accumulating enough observations. "If you work with people enough and get to know them − even in just the work environment, if you're truly concerned about what makes Joe or Sally tick, you'll probably develop some form of intuitive feel as to what pleases them or you'll sense what's bothering them," says a young executive vice president who got his start in accounting.

Operating in a personal manner improves your chances of making work assignments that permit individuals to derive more satisfaction from their jobs. As you learn their interests, avocations, and aspirations, you can do a better job of harmonizing their goals and talents with company goals.

Not all managers are outgoing. For them, it's agonizing to deal personally with employees, especially since they may expect to be in an adversarial relationship with them. They are especially concerned about appearing phony by forcing themselves to do it. And rightfully so. People quickly see through phony attempts. Expressing the sentiments of thousands of workers, a labor union leader suggests to management: "Quit trying to be a buddy; cut out the small talk, such as 'How're the kids?' (when the worker maybe doesn't have any). Tell us what we need to know to do our job. Tell us what you want. Tell us how we're doing."

That's subject matter enough for getting into heart-to-heart talks. You're not out simply to make Joe or Sally feel better; you're trying to learn more about what he or she does. Once you do that, the next step is not too difficult; you *can* make that person feel a little better. As you learn what he or she is doing, you will find something that has been done well, or that went beyond what you expected. A simple compliment can brighten a subordinate's day or week way out of proportion to the token effort on your part.

10
How Managers Manage Themselves

Humanagement does not make a sacrificial lamb of the leader. Today's managers want to manage both themselves and their situations in order to be effective and to satisfy their own needs for individualism, self-fulfillment, and meaningful work and relationships. Neither effectiveness nor satisfaction can be gauged by how many things a manager attends to in a given period of time or how many hours he or she slaves at them. People who visit top executives are sometimes surprised at how little these busy leaders seem to do — how clean their desktops are. They fail to see the careful definition of duties and the good delegation that go into an executive's not looking overworked.

Productive managers apply their intelligence, experience, and creativity as often as necessary to maximize the effectiveness of the activities they are overseeing. It is difficult to determine when managers may be applying these personal resources. The work doesn't always look like work. They may mull over a matter during the evening, in the shower, or even on the golf course. Not all problems are neatly structured and not all solutions fall into place on call.

On the other hand, what looks like work isn't always effective, productive, management work. It's easy to fall victim to administrivia — paperwork that can pile up faster than you can work through it. And there are people to talk with and meetings to attend — not all of which are productive.

Fred is president of a medium-sized manufacturing company. A page from his desk calendar shows the variety of work he faces:

Things to do today:

7:30 Bi-monthly meeting with plant foremen.

8:15 Talk with secretary about performance, pay raise.

8:30 Meet with vice presidents of marketing and engineering for preliminary look at new line of business.

9:30 Meet with local officials re rumor of plant closing (to which there is some truth).

10:30 Talk with vice president of manufacturing — why he is resigning (would really need him here if we enter new line of business).

11:00 Work on notes for speech at marketing association meeting.

12:00 Lunch — bank officials — establish new line of credit in the event of launching new business.

1:30 Drive to Hampton with sales manager and —

2:00 Talk with key customer re high reject rate on parts we have been shipping them.

3:30 Back to office — pick up tickets and itinerary for West Coast trip — meet with capital appropriations committee, final decision needed on adding material handling equipment vs. replacing turret lathe.

4:30 Meet with pension fund managers, discuss changes required by new legislation.

5:00 More work on speech notes.

6:30 Organization dinner — Boy Scout fund-raising campaign.

Sometime — preferably morning — check progress on repair of heat-treating furnace.

If the phone doesn't ring and no employees or outside visitors pop in, the day should fit together pretty well for Fred. There are other important things he should tend to, but his list for the day covers about all the key matters he can handle.

The trouble is, there will be interruptions. That time for speech writing will probably disappear (and he'll write it at home late tonight). At least one of the meetings will run short or fall through; he'll be stuck with some unexpected free time, but this too will disappear. Another meeting is bound to run long, keeping someone waiting or forcing him to reschedule the meeting that was to have been next. An untold number will phone him or come to his office. Most managers find that a schedule of plan-of-the-day falls apart from the time they arrive at work. That's why the majority don't even try to live by a schedule.

THE ROUTINE AND THE UNEXPECTED

The shearing action of routine versus unexpected tasks can be devastating — or exciting. Planned or unplanned, the variety of challenges that present themselves in a day's work is the very thing that some managers thrive on. Ask any executive what the principle benefits of the job are, and chances are that freedom and variety will come out high on the list. Being uncomfortable with repetitive, routine work is the mark of people who carry heavy responsibilities in management. Ask a lower or middle manager what the worst aspect of his or her job is and it will probably have something to do with having too much paperwork or too much routine.

A manager probably not only prefers an open schedule, but the job may demand that this person be fairly free-wheeling. Open time is needed because so much of the real work is concerned with the unexpected. Not all the problems to be contended with can be written into an appointment book.

When some aspects of a job become routine, a manager has more time to devote to the essentials, to make himself more effective. The key is to recognize that this added time is gradually becoming available and invest it rather than simply padding out the day. When a training manager found one of his courses was becoming routine and he realized that he had slipped into a costly pattern of traveling all over the country to conduct it, he assembled the updated material into a self-teaching package and mailed it out instead. His departmental budget savings for the year were unbelievable. By breaking a routine work habit, he was able to cut travel expenses and go on to newer, more important activities.

Some managerial jobs are totally unstructured. These managers live from crisis to crisis, reacting to events rather than managing them. Though any manager may have to play "firefighter" now and then, if the job is constantly dictated by other people and unexpected events, he or she is not really managing. Such a manager, or perhaps senior management, should restructure the job and, possibly, other parts of the organization.

Working long hours is sometimes the style at a particular organization. And it becomes contagious. Some companies give the impression that they expect managers to work long hours six or seven days a week. More and more managers are insisting, however, that compliance with that sort of routine isn't the mark of success. It may be the way to get ahead in that company, but it isn't necessarily the best way to manage. One effective manager says he plans the week out in general terms and establishes checkpoints so he knows where he stands. He works as long a day as necessary, but he will not carry a briefcase home. Another says, "I've simply made it a rule, and enforce it on myself, that I will not work overtime or Saturdays on routine matters. Those managers who regularly come in Saturdays because they aren't bothered by the phone ringing are only rationalizing. They aren't organized."

Management of their own time is one of the most difficult tasks for managers. Increased attention to the people factors and the proliferation of "outside" factors on business intensify this traditional problem. They must continually redefine just what it is that they are supposed to accomplish and then find the most effective manner of tending to the basics.

One of the human frailties that gets in the way is the tendency for managers — like anyone else — to do what they enjoy most. This does not always coincide with the job that has to be done. In the face of complex challenges, it is more comfortable to get bogged down in work that they like but should be delegating. They get satisfaction from doing things themselves and getting quick feedback. To avoid that trap, some managers designate specific amounts of time, if not a specific time of day, for attending to critical tasks. Some keep a log of how they spend their time or have a secretary monitor their activities for a week or so. This information gives them a basis for determining which activities need more time and which are wasting their time.

Some managers get bogged down in detail because they let their subordinates delegate in reverse. To serve their egos, they will take on anybody's work, particularly if they see it as a challenge. A young, competent design engineer for a high-technology company was a master at getting others to do things for him. Frequently, when he had an assignment he couldn't handle, he would ask one of his buddies in the toolmaking department to design and make the item. On one occasion, however, he was unable to get anyone to design a small tool that was needed. An older, now retired, design engineer who supervised the department recalls that it was a relatively minor assignment, but several days went by and the younger man hadn't completed the drawing.

"I got a call from upstairs wanting to know why the design hadn't been sent to the tooling department," the senior engineer says. "I told them I'd send it through as soon as I received it. Then I went to check up on this young fellow to find out why it was taking so long. I looked at the sheet of paper on his drawing board and noticed that all he had done in three days was to draw a horizontal line." Two more days went by and again the older engineer went to check on the young man's progress. "He still had nothing on that paper but a horizontal line. So I took the request sheet from him and did the design myself. It took about 15 minutes. Some years later, the young man was promoted to the job of chief design engineer. I guess they figured the thing he was best at was getting other people to do the work — so they promoted him."

One thing not included in a manager's job description is re-doing unsatisfactory work of subordinates. The manager is supposed to get performance from the subordinate — and, if necessary, to develop that person's ability to perform. The manager has other responsibilities to fulfill; a manager who re-does the work of subordinates is likely to find himself continually pulled away from more essential duties. Having another subordinate re-do a poor job is not the solution, because the person who originally did it will not learn how it should have been done and the person stuck with the re-work will be disgruntled at having to clean up someone else's mistakes. The key to the manager's managing his own time, in this case, is developing or dismissing the troublemaker.

ESTABLISHING PRIORITIES

For the sake of developing others and for controlling the demands on their own time, managers have to let assistants, key subordinates, and secretaries know exactly what their primary duties and objectives are. These workers should be helping the manager accomplish these duties — quite the reverse of *their* delegating details *to* him or her. This means managers must first establish in their own minds what the priorities are. Most effective managers set priorities on the many activities before them because they know that effectiveness means doing the right job. They feel more comfortable working from a priority list than from a daily schedule, because it provides the flexibility they need and keeps their attention on the critical aspects of the job. The managers most likely to put off crucial decisions and let problems fester are those who never take the time to step back and analyze their jobs or envision what they ought to be doing.

Priorities have to be set not only according to the relative importance of tasks but in terms of completion date and starting date. Some work is due to be completed soon and obviously has to be started soon — today, if not yesterday. But long-range work can be deceiving. While the completion date may be far off, the initial work cannot always be delayed; some things may have to be done immediately. A manager generally is expected to handle both long-range and short-range assignments, as well as those continuous functions that never go away. Mixing the timing factor with the relative importance factor means the manager may have to make the decision as to whether to work on the short-term, low-priority task or to begin the long-term, high-priority work. To keep the priority list meaningful, the manager constantly has to update it. Studying corporate goals as well as his or her particular objectives, analyzing opportunities, and detecting weak spots in the organization, the manager determines which items should be added to the list, be removed, or be changed in ranking.

Although you can identify something as top priority, only occasionally can you work on it to the exclusion of everything else. A manager has to keep several balls in the air at once, giving undivided attention to a problem for a short time, making a decision or getting people working on one, and then going on to the next matter.

A manager's activities may be governed to a large degree by deadlines. Sometimes crucial ventures, sometimes relatively minor chores, these activities do have completion dates which force their way onto the priority list. Generally, managers consider their assigned deadlines fair. Occasionally, however, they are handed deadlines that seem unreasonable or unrealistic either in terms of being met at all or being met with good, sound work. When that happens, some have no reservations about discussing the problem with their supervisors. If circumstances don't permit changing an unreasonable completion date, some managers will comply to the best of their abilities, indicating the handicaps under which they and their people have performed. When a subordinate tells them a deadline assigned by someone up the line is unreasonable, they determine why it can't be met and what, if anything, can be changed so that it can be met. If they conclude that the situation is impossible, they are then armed with the information needed to march upstairs to negotiate some flexibility.

SETTING UP A SCREEN

How managers define their jobs to others and how they manage their time are determined considerably in the reporting procedures they establish. They shape their jobs as they determine the number of persons reporting to them, the type of information they want, and the decisions which they insist on making. In each manager's day-to-day operating style, he can express priorities and delineate those things he wants no part of if a screen of key people is set up. This device will filter out enough irrelevant or unimportant intrusions on the manager's time to permit him to handle high-priority business. A screen may consist merely of one secretary, or it may include a number of assistants or subordinate managers. Some executives prefer to screen all their activities through one trusted executive assistant.

In the more military-style hierarchy, an executive would have one assistant or two deputies reporting to him. No one else would get through the screen except on urgent matters. Modern business organizations have expanded this screen, but have established an unwritten rule that a manager should have no more than six or seven persons reporting to him. Today, however, some managers have as many as 20 others reporting to them. Cornell Maier, president of Kaiser Aluminum and Chemical Corporation, operates in this "flat management concept." While he can counsel each of these managers on their operational problems and set goals with them, he has allowed himself no choice but to let them run their own shows.

Since the amount of information available to a manager is skyrocketing, he must also establish a screen for written material. The manager must decide, and make known to the staff, what is wanted and the form in which it is wanted. Otherwise, the manager will be so overloaded that essentials that relate to established priorities for action will be missed.

Screening the people who come to your office is more difficult. Most managers believe firmly in an open-door policy. They regard the closed door as a barrier to communications with peers and subordinates. They want everyone in the company to feel they are welcome at any time, although they may realize that unrestricted access leaves them open to matters that cut deeply into their effectiveness. The open door can encourage communication about nonessentials; many people accept it as an invitation to drop in for friendly, non-business talks. (However, what starts out as apparently pointless discussion may sometimes be a person's way of leading into more important matters — either professional or personal.) At the same time, people who should be coming in may not do so; they may not have time to wait in line. The open door policy does not guarantee good communications.

Setting a tone of openness and informality works well in most management situations. But a manager may want to limit what this means in terms of access to his office. A manager may prefer to make himself available at the time he selects. When out and about the plant or office and encountering someone who merits more time and greater privacy, he can then set up an appointment in the office.

Screening telephone calls is much easier, and many managers have no qualms about doing it. Their secretaries block interruptions by people selling raffle tickets and office supplies, redirect calls that can be better handled by someone else in the company, "bank" calls to more appropriate times when they are less busy, and rush urgent calls through.

Some managers — busy or not — have their secretaries employ the old "he's out of the office" trick. There's nothing wrong, however, with the honest explanation: "He has someone in his office" or "He is writing a report and does not wish to be disturbed until. . . " The straight answer lets people know you have work to do and that placing a phone call to you doesn't automatically win an audience. You may tell your secretary that you are not going to take any phone calls for a certain period of time; people can either call again or leave word to be called. This leaves you free from interruptions and establishes a block of time for getting things done by phone. One manager feels that since the phone usually works *for* rather than *against* him, he generally answers calls himself. But for those busy times, he buzzes his secretary to intercept calls. Sometimes he punches the buzzer all day long and other days not at all.

Managers who answer their own phones don't consider it disruptive, or, if they do, they figure the price is worth it. They don't like to encounter screening on the calls they make. They also fear that having their calls screened might discourage people from calling them. Some are adept at quickly transferring many of the calls they get to subordinates who are better prepared to handle the matter.

The screening process can be overdone. It can insulate you from the essentials that you should be dealing with — inside the company or outside. Eating in private dining rooms, flying in the company plane, and surrounding yourself with a few subordinates who block access by others, you may get no view, or only a distorted view, of the outside world. Effective executives are masters at acquiring information in a variety of ways. They read, discuss, listen to reports, meet with people outside their industries, and sound out anyone from cabdrivers to shareholders. Within their organizations, they respectfully zig and zag around channels to tune in on what people think and feel. Although they are protected by a screen, they use it as an offensive formation so they can take the initiative in getting in touch with people and collecting information.

SUBORDINATES MAKE THEIR OWN DEMANDS

One person who always has access to you is your boss. And your effectiveness depends heavily on how he or she defines your work —

what you do and how you do it. Furthermore, your boss is in the best position to provide feedback on how effectively you are managing. Managers who do well generally admire their bosses. They respect and like them on a professional basis and, quite likely, on a personal basis as well. They credit much of their professional development to the example and coaching of the person they work for. Over the years, surveys by *Industry Week* have shown that two out of three managers rate their relations with their supervisors as "good" and the rest call them "satisfactory." Nearly nine out of ten speak favorably of the performance of the person to whom they report.

It's as important to study your boss as it is to learn your job. Like most people, any boss can be influenced by little things such as the way people dress, how often they smile, and their tactfulness in expressing disagreement. If you respect your boss, think his or her goals are worthwhile, and feel you can be part of the team working toward those goals, don't let little things stand in the way of getting the big job done. But, with most bosses, the important things do count first. There are several things they want from a subordinate manager:

- Knowledge of your job and how to handle it.

- Objective reports on what's going on in your area.

- Solutions rather than problems.

- Warning of potential major problems and your suggested solutions.

There is danger in doing no more than what the boss expects or demands. A dynamic follower will do some demanding of his own. We have traditionally assumed that it's the boss's responsibility to cause the work group to function well, says William J. Crockett, former vice president, human resources, of Saga Corporation. But the subordinate has an opportunity to make the situation a good one, he asserts.

A dynamic subordinate will press not only to find out what the boss wants done but the manner in which he wants it done, seeking constant feedback and even proposing changes in the job. If you're wise, however, you will stick to what the boss wants until the two of you have agreed to specific changes, says Mr. Crockett.

"You have to obey in general or confront and get things changed. If you can't change them and you don't want to leave, then you ought to obey with grace."

Most managers find that their bosses like to be approached for advice — to be asked for judgment on a decision. But they treat this as a learning device — not as a substitute for making their own decisions. They find it works best if they go to the boss after they have taken action, giving him or her a chance to play "Monday morning quarterback." It's their way of getting the coaching that many bosses will neglect to provide. It's also a way of getting to know the boss's values, goals, and management style — and discovering the ways in which the subordinate and boss are alike and the ways in which they complement each other. They also use their own mistakes as opportunities to see the boss, by saying, "If you've got a little time, I'd like to review what happened because we both know that things went wrong and I'd like your judgment." That's a key word — "judgment." This provides a starting point for discussion and an appeal to a boss's ego.

TRICKS FOR GETTING FEEDBACK

Performance appraisal systems aim at improving managerial effectiveness by having managers set goals for the coming year with their supervisors and review performance toward the past year's goals. By concentrating on performance and skills and avoiding getting into personalities, the supervisor does not have to play psychologist. Nevertheless, these systems require some skillful work by the supervisor and don't always produce good results.

At its best, the performance evaluation produces a written record which provides the subordinate with some idea of how he is doing overall and what his development potential may be. It also provides top management a report on the subordinate's performance, and the subordinate in turn, knows the favorable and unfavorable things they are hearing. Many appraisal systems become lost in forms and process and fail to capitalize on the opportunity for worthwhile coaching sessions. Sometimes the systems become ends in themselves, complain many managers. They see the whole procedure as a paperwork nuisance devised by the personnel department, not as a tool for developing people. Sometimes the system is used principally for the determination of salaries. The appraisal written primarily to justify a salary increase robs the system of its objectivity. Surveys by *Industry Week* indicate that less than half of the managers in industry set or review goals with their supervisors, and that the number has advanced little, if at all, over the last decade.

Even with annual performance appraisals to guide a manager, there are many times when a person wonders how he or she is doing right at the moment. After taking action on a major matter, and perhaps changing the way things are usually done, you are anxious to know what the boss thinks about the validity of your decision. Continual, informal performance feedback reinforces learning as events occur. It permits you to learn *why* you are achieving or failing; the annual appraisal may be too general to be of help.

Ideally, the supervisor uses both systems concurrently, supplementing formal reviews with frequent chats. One manager says he avoids scheduling a meeting with individuals reporting to him because that causes them to tighten up. He simply targets a time to talk with an individual, does some checking around to see that the person is not going to be busy then, and — when the time comes — he invites the person in for a down-to-earth chat.

When the boss simply won't set objectives for a subordinate's work, the subordinate should devise some objectives and then test them on the boss. The boss will respond pretty quickly, agreeing or disagreeing. As a matter of fact, this tactic may help the boss clarify the situation, for he may not have had direct experience in the subordinate's job and would, therefore, appreciate a starting point. The same approach can be used for getting feedback. The subordinate gives the boss a brief progress report — in person or in writing. Even if no more response than "If you don't hear anything from me, you're doing okay" is given, at least the subordinate then knows that the lack of comment is based on awareness of what's happening.

MAKING THE BOSS MORE EFFECTIVE

A manager's effectiveness is partly a matter of how well he or she contributes to the boss's effectiveness. When the boss discusses one of his new projects and you offer to study it, make the computation, write the report, make the contact, or whatever, you help both the boss and yourself. If he accepts your willingness and ability to help, your boss will become comfortably dependent upon you, and you have an opportunity to gain insights into the boss's job.

Generally, you will see only a slice of your boss's full range of responsibilities. You may think that the areas where you and your boss usually interface constitute the most important part of his job, and that may not be the case. You can broaden your view of your boss by seeing him at other than the usual meetings, taking the initiative in bringing relevant matters to his attention, and engaging the boss in discussion of subjects in his other areas of concern. As you try to broaden your perception of the boss, you are taking a risk of being charged with meddling or politicking. Some managers will respond negatively to such efforts; their management style may be to hide behind a formal role and block attempts to be understood.

Your boss's effectiveness depends on many things on and off the job. If you detect that the boss has a problem, you owe it to yourself to answer some questions:

- To whom does your boss report, and what sort of person is that?

- What are your boss's primary responsibilities?

- What are his or her chief successes? How recently have they taken place?

- What are some recent failings that are bothering him or her?

- Who are your boss's enemies?

- What authority does your boss have?

- What responsibilities and authority has your boss delegated? To whom?

- What are his or her major concerns or fears?

- On what basis is your boss being evaluated?

- What does he or she regard as good performance?

- On what basis is your boss evaluating you?

- What aspects of your personality and conduct effect him or her favorably and unfavorably?

As you develop the answers, you can make a fair determination as to whether your boss's problem is personal, job-related, or you. If the problem is personal and you suspect that he or she is not coping with it or not likely to solve it in a reasonable time, you're either going to have to put up with an unhappy — and probably unfair — boss or abandon ship.

If the problem is job-related, you may be able to help. Even if you can't tackle the specific problem for your boss (maybe it's a political battle upstairs), you can cover the areas that have been entrusted to you so well that your boss can devote more energy to the problem.

If you're the culprit, you have another set of questions to pursue. You need to analyze yourself, your job, and your style. People often blame the boss for saying, "This is the way I do things; conform or get out." Yet they operate in a manner that conveys this same attitude: "This is the way I work; take me or leave me. I made the last boss happy this way; it ought to be good enough for you."

Your relationship to the boss is basically an opportunity to help. The more your goals mesh, the better you can work together. If your good performance helps your boss's performance, you can find satisfaction in this job and improve your odds for promotion by pushing him upward. On the other hand, the supervisor who is not promotable may resent a promising subordinate. The better you perform, the more you will be feared — unless your boss is one of those few who will take pride in helping others move up and beyond.

The boss has delegated certain responsibilities to you, and you are expected to be accountable for them. "The dynamic subordinate," Mr. Crockett has found, "not only fully and cheerfully performs this function of accountability, but he initiates it. The subordinate who can do this with unlimited and uninhibited trust makes his boss his advocate — his partner — and gains additional trust and freedom."

The boss who isn't interested in all the details leaves you in a position to run things the way you choose. But if he wants to keep a close hand on things, it's smart to invite your boss to visit your operation frequently and talk with your people. That doesn't mean, though, that your boss should undermine you by making your people come directly to him for decisions.

Keeping the boss informed is fundamental to supporting him. Yet one of the most common violations of the boss-subordinate trust is the tendency to slant or modify reports to make them seem favorable, to present half-truths, or to conveniently forget to mention something that went wrong. People sometimes do this under the guise of shielding the boss from problems that would needlessly disturb him In the long run, this practice hurts both your boss and the organization. Your boss can't correct a situation which he doesn't understand or perhaps isn't aware of.

You can also help the boss by playing devil's advocate, providing loyal opposition, and acting as a sounding board for new ideas. But you have to come across as caring and collaborating, not hostile and judgmental. You can do it if you have demonstrated your loyalty and respect in other situations, says Mr. Crockett. You have to have gained your boss's trust for your accuracy and professionalism.

A person's great ideas can sometimes upset a good relationship with the boss, depending on how the ideas are presented. Excited by the notion of selling a great idea, a manager rushes to the boss and goes off half-cocked with too little information, too little analysis, and too little time to state the case. A more systematic manager loads up for weeks, then calmly walks in and fires both barrels, figuring that no intelligent person could turn the idea down. Both approaches stand a good chance of rejection.

The successful innovator thinks long and hard about both the idea and the boss. It's one thing to have a new idea; to sell it means knowing the customer's needs, as any good salesman will attest. If you know the boss's problems, goals, and needs, you can then direct your approach to showing how you can help. This demands far more work than the half-cocked approach and avoids pinning the boss to the wall as the double-barrel approach does. By appealing to some key concerns of the boss, you offer neither too much nor too little. Letting your boss see how the idea solves one of his problems doesn't force him into a defensive position in which he feels compelled to search for some weak points in your proposal.

Even the best approach may fail. This doesn't mean that you're all wrong, but you may need to do some more thinking before you present your case again. It's quite possible that you don't have as broad a view of the situation as the boss does. Or your failure may have been a matter of poor timing. Maybe you haven't left him sufficient room to make some of the proposal his "own idea." To varying degrees, people want some of their own brand on a worthwhile development. Sometimes, the idea you fail to sell to the boss today becomes his great idea next year. Until your idea is accepted, you have to live with your boss's decision.

Quite often, a touchy relationship with the boss is the result of a lot of little things. If you break them down and tackle one at a time, you may be able to resolve them. Each boss has a particular, complex blend of strengths and weaknesses. He may be young and new at the job, or so busy trying to figure out what his own job is that there's no time to become familiar with the details of yours. Or the boss may be stale in the job, having long ago abandoned any objectives beyond keeping things on an even keel.

13 SIGNS OF A BAD SITUATION

If wide differences between you and the boss persist, one or both of you will have to change. If that seems to present a stalemate, it's not — you lose. The subordinate gets hurt when there is a big gap in values, say experienced managers.

The odds are high that a bad relationship is ruining your performance and your chances for getting promoted to a more comfortable situation if your boss:

1. Takes sole credit for things you've accomplished.
2. Prefers talking about the one wrong decision you made more than the nine right ones.
3. Tells you you're doing something poorly, but refuses to define how and why.

4. Takes honest disagreement as a personal attack.
5. Isn't passing objective information on your performance up the line.
6. Jumps in every time a slightly unusual problem comes up.
7. Makes a practice of holding private conversations with your subordinates.
8. Reprimands you in front of your subordinates or peers.
9. Doesn't understand your job and refuses to discuss your goals and performance.
10. Has retired on the job or given up the battle.
11. Expends more effort in hiding mistakes than pushing for progress.
12. Is miles apart from you in ethical standards or management tactics.
13. Thinks you are miles apart in ethical standards or management tactics.

A serious test of your relationship comes when you are pulled into a political situation by your boss. He or she may, for example, refuse to follow directions, forcing you to choose whether to support top management or join in thwarting them. Veterans advise: if you think the boss has chosen better objectives and acceptable tactics for achieving them, join forces with your boss in an *open* disagreement with top management; if you honestly think the boss is wrong, say so. In making either alliance, openness is the best insurance against losing. You may not win the battle, but at least you will not have entered a war which you are bound to lose. Openness will draw the lines for honest disagreement and command the respect of those with whom you disagree. If you and the boss lose to upper management, you have at least shown loyalty to your boss and open, fair disagreement with management. No one should fault you for that. If the boss loses and you have sided with management, you should be respected for your open disagreement. However, if the boss resents your "disloyalty," the race is on to see whether you will be cut down before top management can pull you up.

When you run afoul of your boss, you had better be ready to put your job on the line. Hammering away at your own performance will, in the long run, best prepare you to move ahead either in your present organization or in another one. Having studied your boss, you should be able to anticipate whether he would overlook your differences and reward you for performance or undercut you. If you think he will respond vindictively, be set to leave — without a good recommendation from him to your next employer.

One of the ironies of today's more professional-type managers is their willingness to put their jobs on the line in order to do what they think is right. Many are willing to risk being fired in order to perform the best they can and to prepare for carrying greater responsibilities. They take their work too seriously to be turned off or turned aside by their bosses or anyone else.

They run the risk, even when they are entirely right, of neglecting to make small sacrifices to build strong personal relationships, however. When they disagree with their boss, some people forget they are dealing with a sensitive human being. One young manager — one of the "tell it like it is" generation — got into a straightforward discussion with his boss. He made numerous critical, personal comments, believing they were necessary to clarify his argument. During the hour of discussion, the supervisor wilted visibly, slouching into his chair. Finally, he sat up and blurted, "Hey! Take it easy! I've got feelings, too!"

11
People in Motion

Motion has been part of the morality of modern industrialized life. The individual who stays in one job and performs it the same way year after year is generally not regarded as a success. "Success" is more likely to depend on how far and how fast you rise in the corporate hierarchy. In recent years, success has also been attributed to the person who moves from company to company, continually "doing better."

For most of the industrial era, however, companies promoted people of proven company loyalty, not only because loyalty was a quality valued by management, but because long-term employment with the company was the means of developing competence. A manager would rise within a certain company, developing skills at the company's expense, learning how to manage from those who promoted him. How else but on the job could a person learn what the company wanted done and how to do it "the company way?"

Today, with companies more diversified and open to better ways of managing, and with the portable skills and techniques of managers, mobility can contribute to developing both the individual and a management team with a breadth of viewpoints and experience. Many companies have found advantages in moving people over from the "wrong" columns of the organization chart, across functional lines, and from other companies — even from other industries.

"The modern thinking is that the broader your background, the more valuable you'll be to the company," says one veteran manager who has worked in three different industries. The new logic for many people, then, is: Mobility brings competence; competence is replacing loyalty as the basis for advancement; therefore, mobility is the way to get ahead.

The trap in this line of thinking is "competence." Mobility can guarantee nothing but motion. Whether it leads to competence depends on how the individual makes use of his or her mobility. Growth, not movement, builds competence.

Mobility may mask a person's inner unhappiness. For some managers, the upward ascent takes them to places where they are uncomfortable and unfulfilled. And for those who are rising swiftly to broader responsibilities, motion and promotion can sometimes lull them into slackening their efforts to learn. Thinking, "I'll only be here for two years," a mover may try to look good without rocking the boat. The company may lose in the long run when a manager concentrates on the short term, neglecting the considerations that will turn sour long after he or she has passed on to a higher position. Such a manager may produce good quarterly earnings reports by neglecting investment in new facilities, maintenance, research and development, advertising, and people development. This stepping-stone game causes inestimable damage to corporate effectiveness and well-being.

Some top executives believe a subtle weakness is overtaking industry because of too much intercompany mobility. The mobile manager with portable skills can bring new know-how to a job, but he or she may lack something that many corporations have lost sight of. The so-called professional manager may fail to develop enough expertise about a particular business or product line to become a leader or innovator; common-denominator knowledge is valuable, but managers need a special insight that comes from knowing the technology of that particular business.

NO GUARANTEES OF COMPANY LOYALTY

Loyalty to the company is no longer the restraint on mobility that it once was. The executive who no longer feels challenged or adequately compensated will head for another employer. On the other hand, he or she may wind up on the street because the job suddenly is no longer needed; that person's expertise was secured only for a particular time.

The individual who marches into an office on the assumption that he is settling down to a 30-year deal is a rarity and may be in for disappointment somewhere along the way. Some people call loyalty a treacherous, one-way street. Instead of a glowing retirement dinner, they suggest that a more likely farewell consists of a once-revered executive being ingloriously ejected from the very building that bears his name. Realists believe simply that a company owes a person nothing more than a paycheck for the last day's work and can release an individual whenever it likes. And yet the individual considering a career change must do so in complete secrecy!

A more objective look at loyalty puts it into the perspective of responsibility or vested interest. The individual manager and the company accept certain responsibilities toward one another. Their relationship broadens and deepens with time, each giving something to the other so that a mutual vested interest develops. Instant, automatic, blind loyalty makes no sense for today's employee, however. Loyalty can, and often does, come into the picture in time, but it's not the loyalty of old.

Companies themselves have done many things that have fostered mobility and laid company loyalty to rest. Those that regularly go outside to hire key executives are on soft ground when they demand loyalty from their people. There are still a few companies which maintain that they promote only from within, but even some of them will hire a manager from the outside when the chips are down. This "betrayal" of the closed, loyal community can stir others to leave the company.

Company loyalty has undoubtedly been dampened by the transiency of companies. They, too, undergo turnover. The company to which an individual pledged his or her allegiance 30 years ago may now have been acquired by another company, which, in turn, was acquired by another. The people, the objectives, the location, and the work atmosphere may all have changed dramatically. Eventually, an employee finds that nothing to which he once attached himself is there any longer. What choice is there, then, but to put up with disappointment – or change employers? Young managers can see that it doesn't pay to attach your life to a corporate entity that can make no guarantee that it will reciprocate.

An organization built on tender offers and named by a computer or public relations counsel offers little tradition to which the employee can attach. Hopes of possibly building a future together are clouded by the likelihood of further rounds of conglomerization and concentration of business organizations. People prefer, then, to pin their loyalty on a company that is successful — both in terms of profits and in public image. But their loyalty is conditional. As long as they have challenging content in their jobs, competitive compensation, and the opportunity for professional development, they will reciprocate with dedication to corporate goals. Along the way, they often develop genuine loyalties to particular supervisors or associates. But even these personal bonds will not hold a manager from moving to another company.

Surveys by *Industry Week* show the percentage of managers who have been hired from another firm to their present position increased to 27 percent in 1975 from 22 percent in 1965. The surveys also show an increase in the percentage of managers who have serious doubts as to whether they'll be with their present employer in five years. This number rose from 21 percent in 1965 to 30 percent in 1975. It is particularly significant that people who have been promoted within their firms are becoming more willing to consider employment in other companies.

A special *Industry Week* survey on industry line-crossing revealed that 70 percent of the respondents have not ventured outside the industry in which they were first employed. That doesn't mean they haven't thought seriously about switching. Two-thirds of those managers who have not switched have considered it, and most of them still might do so. For nearly eight out of ten who have made the cross-over, a key reason is the inability to achieve personal goals on their previous job.

Disappearance of the stigma that once went with changing jobs permits people to seek positions that are more rewarding in terms of pay, more fulfilling work, or less demanding work. The trend is no more a guarantee of happiness than it is a sign of unhappiness. A manager who is not necessarily unhappy may decide to accept a better offer. Rising expectations propel people to look constantly for even greener grass. On the other hand, a non-mobile manager may be quite unhappy. Reluctance to give up retirement benefits and other fringe benefits tied to longevity make it hard to move, creating a locked-in feeling.

CAREERISM IN A NEW LIGHT

The frustration or locked-in feelings of the person who is not moving up or out of his or her present position often stems from corporate and societal definitions of success — not the individual's. But all the books on how to get ahead in management may become irrelevant to many younger managers and would-be managers. In their drive for self-fulfillment, they are putting success into their own terms. They will not be boxed in by someone else's definition of success. Some will choose to work their way up the corporate ladder, but few will allow themselves to be pushed. And those who decline will not be shamed.

By chaining people to ladders of progression, the corporation sets up incentives and measures of success which don't match everyone. Career ladders serve neither the individual nor the corporation well, says Dr. Frederick Herzberg. No matter where they are on the corporate ladder, people should be able to make use of their growing wisdom. We should design work so that people are not considered obsolete simply because they do not move up to a higher position in the hierarchy.

Too often, careerism has been confused with accomplishment, says Dr. Herzberg. The careerist, he explains, lives his life as a collection of single dimensions, keeping his work divorced from his family, his leisure activities, and his social relationships. An accomplisher, by contrast, finds significance in his work which relates to his whole life; everything he does is in harmony. The careerist cares for his career; the accomplisher, for his work.

Realizing that neither mobility nor "moving up" are guarantees of accomplishing what they want, people are more frequently passing up promotions. This suggests that the time is not far off when corporations will have to adjust their incentives to foster an atmosphere in which individuals can develop their potential, grow personally, and find satisfaction without having to move upward or change companies.

This is not a hopeless challenge. There is already a good base on which to build. One recent survey showed that 63 percent of managers in industry derive "good" satisfaction from their work; 32 percent find it adequate. Only 5 percent call it "poor."

People's values have changed dramatically over recent years. Status is giving way to meaningful personal relationships, titles are yielding to significant work as an incentive, and people realize that promotions and pay increases are not the only measures of personal worth. Their inner peace is likely to depend on how they answer such questions as:

- Do I have access to the company's decision-making apparatus?
- Am I always involved in decisions that I will be responsible for carrying out?
- Does the company give me the satisfaction of participating in policy-making at the highest possible level for my position?
- Does my boss keep me continually challenged?
- Is my boss interested in my welfare and development?
- How is the company treating others who are in positions parallel to mine?
- When I know what the boss would do in a given situation, do I have the authority to do it without asking?
- Does the company allow me to make the contributions I want to make?

WHAT ATTRACTS MANAGERS MOST?

When managers are asked why they selected their present employer, the most frequent response is "challenge." (Money and geographic location lag far behind in a virtual tie for second place.) About four out of five managers indicate in *Industry Week* surveys that they want a position of greater responsibility; they want to grow and develop. Whether they do anything about it is another matter. But many are willing to change employers in their search for challenge — more challenge than they find in their present jobs or expect to encounter in the foreseeable future.

Some managers — four out of ten — feel unchallenged because their present jobs do not permit them to make full use of their capabilities. (Yet any manager worth his or her salt would not admit to an inability to contribute more.) It is possible that managers who say they have to look elsewhere for challenge are referring to the prospects for advancement. Only about two out of ten feel their opportunity to advance to a higher position in their company is good. Twice as many feel the opportunity is poor. The surveys do not reveal, however, just how many of these managers are suited for moving up.

It is a fact of life that the pyramid does get smaller at the top. When survey respondents comment on their prospects for advancement, they may be reflecting on their personal chances — not a situation in which no one moves up. In this age, when the drive for personal fulfillment is being expressed so strongly, the traditional corporate pyramid permits only a select few to find fulfillment and gives other good people little choice but to seek the top of another pyramid. If organizations were less hierarchical, they could better harness the talents that now flounder in meaningless mobility.

Not everyone who changes employers does so to make a big step upward in pay and responsibility. A person may move to a rather similar position strictly for greater financial compensation. Or he may settle for little or no financial gain at all in order to take a job that is more meaningful or challenging. For many people who job-hop, the change can mean a small step upward, when remaining with their present employers means either no movement or a step that is too big for them. A manager with some potential to rise further may not have all the capabilities needed for the next job up the line in his or her company, but a move outside may provide a more suitable increment of improvement.

Some of the impetus for changing companies comes from inadequate recognition. About one-fourth of the managers in industry say they do not get adequate recognition of their accomplishments. When it is granted, recognition too often comes on a hit-or-miss basis. A manager may be praised one day for something that he thinks is relatively insignificant and wonder the next day why the boss hasn't said anything about his performance on a really critical project or a highly innovative suggestion.

Poor handling of performance appraisal and recognition are costly to the corporation. While 30 percent of the managers surveyed by *Industry Week* doubt that they will be with their present employer five years from now, the incidence is double that among managers who feel shortchanged in recognition.

This search for recognition, say some experts, partially explains why so many managers enroll in formal courses in management. In 1965, only 46 percent of the respondents to an *Industry Week* survey said they had enrolled in a formal management course in the past two years. By 1975, course enrollees had jumped to 63 percent. Ironically, companies that provide or support such courses create high expectations among their managers and lay the groundwork for high mobility. People will change jobs if they think they are being developed for opportunities that don't exist.

MANAGEMENT MISMATCHES

Contrary to the popularized concept of the business world portrayed in books and movies, ungainly or unpopular organizations are usually not the design of evildoers or corporate monsters. Generally, they are the sum of myriad small mistakes, often made with the best of intentions by people who have been placed in the wrong positions.

A fundamental reason for the frequent mismatches of managers and responsibilities and for the under-utilization of management talent is the fact that management is an undeveloped profession. The individual doesn't know what he or she has in terms of what's needed, and the managers who select and promote others don't know what they're looking for or how to find it.

Management often selects a person for its ranks because he does well in a functional specialty. It either doesn't consider or has not had an opportunity to observe this person's people-management skills. Even when management is considering experienced managers for promotion, mistakes can be made. Looking only at a person's past successes can be misleading. Taking someone who is successful and trying to make him more successful, may push him beyond his ability to perform because a person's strengths and weaknesses depend on the particular situation. A manager may not perform as effectively in one position as he did at another time and place. Management has to know both the individual and the specifics of the job in order to select properly. But management jobs are not easily defined — especially in advance. That's why some less-structured companies succeed through selecting good people and letting them shape their own positions within certain parameters.

Management mismatches are provoked, too, by the many people who want to be managers and shouldn't be, or by those who aspire to higher positions than they are suited for. Some are attracted to management because managing other people looks like a higher order of existence than they can attain in their present jobs. Power, status, and pay attract people whose talents do not lie in managing. There are companies, however, where specialists or professionals in non-management positions can earn many of the same benefits as managers. In the last few years, some companies have established dual lines of progression that permit a person — a salesman or research scientist, for example — to advance in pay and recognition on a par with his management cohorts, but without leaving his specialty.

Being in a place that's wrong for you — not the situation *per se* — is the cause of tenseness, says California psychologist Roger Gould. People under the most job stress are often forced to act quite differently on the job than they do on their own time. Their lives are segmented. For them, work constitutes a loss of self rather than realization of self.

Under the best of circumstances, a manager works against pressure, striving to meet standards set both by himself and by his supervisors. Managers must submit to tensions in their relationships with subordinates and peers, with competitors and customers, with stockholders and community leaders. Unless an individual is suited for meeting the challenges of the job, he is likely to change course to avoid conflict, surrender to avert problems, and possibly still dash his personal life to pieces. Those who are well-matched to the job, however, seem to thrive on what looks like stress to bystanders.

Indications are that the divorce rate, alcoholism, heavy smoking, illness, and other manifestations of stress are no higher among business executives than among other groups. In fact, psychologists think they might even run lower because they tend to be balanced individuals — acting much the same on the job as they do at home. For them, work is not a loss of self. In general, stress propels them to accomplishment. In times when it threatens to become too much, they find releases.

Few situations put more pressure on a manager than labor contract negotiations. Jack G. Hall, labor counsel for Dart Industries, Inc., normally sews up seven to ten contracts a year. He logs 140,000 to 170,000 miles in airplanes to do it — a pace that keeps him at the bargaining table or in a hotel room more than in his Los Angeles office. Years ago, at 30, he recalls, he left a bargaining session and found that he couldn't climb the three flights of stairs to his room in the hotel. "I was frightened. I immediately cancelled everything and headed for home and the doctor's office. There was nothing wrong with my heart," he learned. "My doctor told me I was simply tied in knots with tension, and that I either had to learn to live with it or get out of that business."

Mr. Hall then built in enough pressure valves to survive. The key was to gain confidence in himself, recognize the good support he got from management, and not interpret failure to reach all of management's bargaining objectives as personal defeat or a lack of skill. His previous health problems disappeared.

WINDING UP AND UNWINDING

The effective, hard-charging executive today is rarely the work-to-the-exclusion-of-everything-else person. He or she may "wind up" to be able to tackle challenges on the job, but makes sure to unwind at every opportunity. Good managers control their corporate life to make time available for themselves. Their social life is not tied to corporate-related activities. Clubby social obligations that might let business intrude on privacy are shunned. For people who commit themselves to being key members of an organization, "privacy" is a new but important consideration.

An increasing percentage of managers never entertain business associates at home, or do so infrequently. They rarely entertain colleagues from the company. Home entertaining is reserved for close friends. Big parties are a bore. The busy manager often doesn't want to discuss business after a hard day at work. Where discussion is the core of a get-together, he prefers to talk with people from other occupations and professions in order to broaden his perspectives. In short, entertaining is a break from, not an extension of, work. In the long run, this may enhance a manager's effectivensss far more than suffering through business talk with business associates. An occasional party with fellow workers helps to see them in another dimension and contribute to good working relationships, but it is not the political arena it once was.

Club membership may help get things done — provide a place for luncheon meetings or facilities for a physical workout that will tone up mind and body for a day of stressful work. Practicality rather than perquisite determines what a manager joins. Where once the plush lobbies and huge leather chairs of a businessman's club constituted a signal that you had made it, the young manager today accepts or rejects such membership on the basis of whether it provides meaningful tools for doing his or her job. Membership *per se* holds little value. If a club bars women members or makes them ride the freight elevator, the modern male manager is apt to scoff at the archaic policies and turn his back on it.

Today's manager tends to shun the traditional status symbols. Compared to his predecessors, he deemphasizes materialism both at home and at work. The male manager takes pride, for example, in getting a suit on sale. Buying one for under $100 is more of an accomplishment than being able to afford a $300 suit, he figures. He doesn't feel the need to give off power images via his attire. He gladly sheds his work "uniform" for a pair of jeans and a sweater, after hours. He keeps office frills to a minimum. He prefers a crudely partitioned office in an old plant, where he can find challenge, to the paneled walls and carpeted floor that decorate a dull job.

Lack of interest in materialism does not mean that a person isn't interested in money. While some new managers may not consume material goods, they may "consume" experiences. Rather than putting money into a lavish automobile, they are apt to spend it on a ski trip or a visit to Disney World. If they need psychic rewards beyond those derived from the job, they turn to sailing, tennis, self-defense arts, scuba diving, racquetball, skiing, or running.

The search for challenge and the insistence on separatism typifies the way many managers approach involvement in civic affairs. Traditionally, businessmen have supported — financially and with manpower — the standing organizations that serve the community. And more do so today than ever. An increasing number of managers, however, will not join an organization simply "because it is there." Often they prefer to lend their support to a non-traditional organization — one in which they have a particular interest and to which they can make a personal commitment. Often, too, they prefer to support a special project, plunging in with all-out dedication until a certain problem has been solved or a goal attained, and then withdrawing.

Businessmen have traditionally lent their names to good causes. It was often part of the job. Along with a particular corporate officership went one's name on the letterhead of certain organizations. Today, the manager is less interested in simply lending his name. He may choose to invest himself, however, and will often apply the resources of the company. But a manager will generally not do so simply on the grounds that it's expected by the company or of the company.

Charles F. Knight, chairman of Emerson Electric Company, is a powerhouse of civic leadership in St. Louis. But, he says, "I'm in on a project basis and when that project's done, I'll be out of it until the next project comes along." Plenty of projects come along for this 42-year-old executive who was awarded *Industry Week's* excellence in management award in 1978 for demonstrating corporate responsibility to the community.

"I get less satisfaction out of getting into institutionalized annual kinds of civic activities even though they are equally important," says Mr. Knight. Some of the projects he tackled in his community include organizing the Save Our St. Louis Sports (SOS) drive that netted high school athletic programs $250,000 — enough to carry them through a one-year crisis; mustering business support for and spearheading a successful school tax increase campaign; developing a Management Assistance Program for studying the school system's operations and money-saving changes; condensing the city's year-long Arts & Education drive into two months and bringing in 40 percent more than had ever been raised; and organizing the area's

Boy Scout recruiting night, which signed up 7000 boys — the largest single recruitment effort by a local scout group anywhere.

Mr. Knight exemplifies the commitment managers can, and do, bring to civic affairs. "Part of my job is making sure the corporation makes a contribution outside of its day-to-day activities of selling and making products. So I view it as an extension of my job."

There is a subtle but important difference between entering civic activities because it's expected of you or the company and doing it because you feel it is fundamental to the role of being a manager. The modern executive is not inclined to hide within the corporate walls, content to make and sell products. He or she blends civic affairs, corporate work, and private life into a satisfying unity.

THE FEMALE REVOLUTION

The changing role of woman in society, with its profound impact on the personal lives of managers and the lives of the people they manage, is altering definitions of success and the conditions of mobility. One of the changes can be seen in the consideration given to the corporate wife. She has traditionally been expected to be an uncomplaining bystander while her husband takes frequent, and sometimes lengthy, business trips or works and entertains long into the night. Periodically, she has been told to pack up, move, and settle her family in a new community where she has no ties and no identity. The problem is not so acute for the husband, who immediately is thrust into his new work, where he meets people, or for the children, who make friends in school. If she does not work outside the home, she may find herself withering away — a victim of rootlessness. One mother of teenagers was struck by the meaning of rootlessness when she realized one day that her neighbors never knew what her children were like when they were growing up.

Traditionally, the wife's dreams and ambitions haven't counted in the face of her husband's. She agreed to provide the emotional cushion for the husband and children. In the later years of marriage, with the children gone and her husband rising high in responsibility and recognition, this worn cushion found herself on the closet shelf.

By the early 1970's, the assertion by women of their need for self-fulfillment was no longer simply a cause or a movement. It was a groundswell of change that affected even those women who were content to hold fairly close to the traditional role of wife and mother. Today, an employer who expects manager's wives to fit into a certain mold meets stiff resistance and unnecessarily complicates the selection and promotion of managers.

A good marriage can help a manager perform well on the job. A bad one can hurt. So an employer has no reason other than social image for insisting that its managers be married, and that consideration carries less and less weight. Not everyone believes that everyone ought to be married. Marriage is not the sign of success that it once was; remaining single carries no stigma other than suggesting homosexuality to some, but even homosexuality is losing some of its stigma. Divorce is increasingly common and therefore more accepted. It's a fact of life, however, that more than nine out of ten managers are married. In the choice between two equally qualified candidates, the married person generally wins over the divorced one. Managers in the process of seeking a new job or a promotion are hurt more by a brewing divorce than the manager already settled in a job. Divorce also hits harder at the upper management levels, since candidates for those jobs are screened more carefully and the family situation is given more weight. Senior managers seem to prefer married managers because matrimony still carries an image of solidity. It also gives them something in common with the younger manager. There might even be a little jealousy involved at times; an older manager might resent the lifestyle of the single or divorced manager who is, or who looks like, a man-about-town.

The working wife has an even more obvious impact on the manager's commitment to job and family. To earn extra income, to escape boredom, or to establish their own identity, an unprecedented proportion of wives are working outside the home. While being a wife, homemaker, and mother has traditionally been the means of fulfillment for women, that is not always the case today. More and more wives from all economic levels are entering the workforce.

Many of these working wives are pursuing careers. Talented and well-educated, they want to prove themselves. Employers have to face the fact that some of their managers have working wives and — furthermore — that some of their managers *are* wives. The simple division of men at work and women at home is fading fast. Dual-career marriages are on the rise and will become quite common, especially among the types of people who enter the management ranks.

At this time, there are few role models for people in dual-career marriages to follow. So far, married career women have generally tried to carry the burden of the domestic tasks as well as their jobs. That is a function not only of their own images of what a working wife should be, but of what society, companies, and the husband expect their role to be. Some husbands do share the household chores and child-raising with their working wives, however. But roles will undergo change in the years ahead.

Dual-career marriages need an extra measure of consideration and understanding. Egos may be bruised when a woman's success on the job outshines that of her husband. For that matter, any degree of self-fulfillment or financial independence may threaten the husband. If he is not secure enough, or if his wife cannot properly carry her success, the husband's ego can deteriorate to the point of sinking the marriage.

Far from abandoning the family in response to demands of the job, a woman executive is apt to go to extreme measures to keep up with family responsibilities. When Margaret Kahliff was president of a small manufacturing company near Cleveland, she always put her family first. Once, when she had to attend a week-long seminar in Chicago, she flew home every night to take care of her small children rather than entrust them to a babysitter.

Companies can no longer assume that when they want to transfer a manager he or she will just pack up and go. A couple may evaluate the offer to see if it works in the best interests of both. If both are employed, they will investigate the possibilities for the partner to find a job that's comparable in present duties, advancement opportunity, compensation, and other benefits. Some women executives worry that they will be passed over for promotion because management assumes they can't move because of their husbands. One woman manager has made a point of telling her boss repeatedly, "Tell me about the opportunity, and I'll tell you if I can move."

That pretty well sums up the emerging attitude of the new breed of managers. They're dealing increasingly for success on their terms.

12
You Can Be What You Want to Be

"I've been so involved in my work lately, it's hard to turn off and go to sleep at night. I'm so wrapped up in our problems, I lie a- wake thinking about what I'm going to do the next day. I'm not worried, and I don't mind it. It's really exciting. In fact, a couple of weeks ago, I turned down an offer for a job that paid much better."

A family man first, Ted does not want to move again. He ac- cepted this job and the move that went with it in order to provide his family better financial security and more time at home than his earlier venture into business for himself. He still works hard. Work is central to his life, but it is not dominant.

Work is central to many people's lives, but it is not the only thing in the center. Unlike their predecessors, for whom work was virtually their total lives, people today do not have to subordinate their personal interests for the sake of economic survival. They de- cide for themselves how their work relates to the rest of their lives. The work ethic is not dead, but people are approaching work on their own terms.

Managers are very much a part of this sweeping social change. While they are work-and-challenge-oriented, they want to achieve *for* themselves, not at the expense of themselves. They work hard at attaining corporate goals when they feel they are simultaneously meeting personal objectives. Their loyalty to themselves and their families ranks at least as high as job loyalty.

Today's manager is not as likely to be driving blindly to the top of the company as managers might have in an earlier generation.

Rising to the top may not be the ultimate goal at all; the new manager's ambitions may be even loftier than that top rung on the corporate ladder. Even managers already at the top may refuse to make a lifelong commitment to the company although they may be devoting 100 percent of themselves to the job.

Each manager is directed by a particular blend of motives to seek economic reward, a sense of accomplishment, and personal identity. Some become workaholics — totally dedicated to their work; much, if not all, of their identity comes from what they accomplish at work or from their association with a particular organization. At the other extreme are those who bide their time, putting up with unfulfilling work because it is a source of income that enables them to seek fulfillment outside the job. But there is growing opportunity for a manager to select a middle ground, where he or she can function as a whole person who finds fulfillment on *and* off the job.

THE SEARCH FOR A FULLER IDENTITY

Jobs have provided people with identity, but, for the most part, this has been a partial identity. Today, people are seeking more meaning and reward than can be found in most jobs. Managers feel that overdependence on the job as a source of self-esteem is something to be avoided, and they are letting employers know that they will either meet these needs in their work or limit their job commitments so they can meet them elsewhere.

Despite the rewarding careers that people have found in management, the work has inherently been difficult to relate to their families. Look at it from the children's point of view: "Daddy (or Mommy) goes to the office. He leaves our world. He gets money for being away. He doesn't bring anything home. Whatever he does during the day, it makes him 'mad' and tired." Not knowing what daddy does can be a problem for the children of any industrial worker, but the manager poses special problems since he ostensibly does something more "important" than others. Important but intangible. While he may take great pride in transacting a sale, guiding the development of a new product, or staying within a tight budget, there is nothing to show the kids.

The manager's work suffers a tarnished image in the family for any one of several reasons. He may truly dislike the work and carry the stress home. Or, liking the work, by long hours away from home or coming home beat from the "rat race," he telegraphs the idea that managing is a miserable occupation. Although the manager may be in control of things at work, his family sees a person who is totally controlled by a job – a person caught in a trap. For quite different reasons, the manager who is enthusiastic about his work can generate a bad image, too. Feeling guilty about enjoying the long hours at work, he talks about how bad the job is. Even if a manager tries to convey enthusiasm to the family, it's hard to explain what he does and why it's exciting. It's easier to exhibit tiredness and frustration. After all, people expect a day's work to be tiring.

In the past, the family breadwinner was a man who demonstrated his love and loyalty to the family by putting his job first. Self-denial was a virtue. But, in this age of self-fulfillment, people are increasingly attentive to their personal needs, and this includes the family's needs – needs beyond basic financial support. As *Industry Week* surveys have shown (see Chapter 5), a manager generally worries about his or her children more than any other personal or professional consideration. People don't want to earn the family's love and respect from a distance, and don't want the definition of who they are to be limited by the work they do. Today's manager would prefer to bring job and family needs together into some meaningful whole. Blocking family matters from disrupting job performance and preventing job concerns from intruding on a happy family life have been a manager's tactics up to now. But managers are changing the way they approach their careers.

The upsurge in people refusing to transfer or be promoted is one sign of increasing priority being given to personal considerations – to fitting work into a bigger context. Corporate management, therefore, is being forced to take a fresh view of its own management corps. In doing so, it may find that the manager who is good at his job but does not make it his whole life may be more objective about the work and more in tune with the people he has to relate to inside and outside the organization. This manager may be more informed and more tolerant. Because he sees beyond the immediate concerns of the daily routine, this manager may expand his role and challenge the company to set higher goals. More entrepreneurial in his approach to a career, he is, not surprisingly, more entrepreneurial and demanding in the role as a manager.

CAREER BLUEPRINTS: PRO AND CON

Free to search for pay, challenge, and identity, a manager has more opportunity than ever to become what he or she wants to be. But a manager has to know how to get it. In order to thrive in an age of humanagement, today's manager cannot simply "float" to success. Now that people can define success in their own terms, they will have to fashion career plans — and life plans — rather than relying on someone else's ladder of progression to guide their efforts.

But managed careers have been the exception rather than the rule. Some people spend more time planning a two-week vacation than planning their careers. They explain that their plan is to "go as high as I can." Yet many admit, in their later years, "I started out aiming at the top but my goals changed." As they progressed toward their goal, they asked themselves: "Am I able to do this? Do I really want to do this?" The answer often turned out to be "no." On the other hand, many executives at the top did not start with the intention or serious hopes of going that far. "Until I was interviewed for the presidency of this company, I had no idea it would happen," confessed H. Robert Sharbaugh when he was chairman of Sun Company. His experience is shared by many chief executives of major corporations.

Many people have attained far higher rank and broader responsibilities than they would have ever dreamed. For some, the result has been a happy one. For others, it has brought discomfort and frustration. They have advanced beyond their capabilities, and the burdens of management weigh too heavily on them.

Is it worth it, then, to chart a career plan? Will it get you where you want to go any faster? Or will it merely serve as a frustrating reminder of unachieved objectives? Will it aim you toward the wrong objectives? Is it better to simply "wing it?"

There are two schools of thought on career planning. It's unquestionably a necessity, say planning advocates. Some of them have gone so far as to put a plan in writing, specifying the position or salary that they will attain in various points in time. Others argue that career planning is a "useless exercise." Some of the nonplanners believe that sizing up the situation periodically and adapting to that is the best way to get to where you want to be. Their thinking is much the same as those planners who admit that one of the biggest mistakes in planning a career is failure to retain some flexibility. A good long-range plan for an organization requires continual updating and adaptation to changing conditions; so does a personal plan. Targeting a specific position or type of work too early in your career may lead you toward the wrong place, since you can't know what being there is really like until you get close — or arrive there. If you realize along the way that you don't have the talent, don't want to cope with the frustrations, or don't want to make the personal and family sacrifices that are involved, it's time to revise your plans and set new targets.

Some people feel they have no need to blueprint their future because they do not hope to become top executives. Obviously, the manager who is not aiming for the presidency has no need to plan a route to it. He or she is free to aim at the position or type of work that fits into a life plan. But that is all the more reason to define a target and attend to the personal development needed to get there. While the pros and cons of career planning can be debated in terms of whether it can help you move upward faster, there is little argument that it can help you become what you want to be — to guide yourself to a spot for which you are best suited. With your sights set on the long-range future, you can better assess the opportunities that arise and determine which will take you where you want to go and which will not serve you well.

Whether they're marching to the presidency or aiming to become the best in some other particular spot, many of today's managers pay attention to their personal growth and renewal. They believe that fulfillment comes not with position so much as with continued self-development. Once you have reached your targeted position, there is a danger of becoming a stagnant, dull person who embarrasses himself, management, and the people who work for him. Goal-setting, then, becomes a matter of finding ways to put new twists into the same old job and blaze new trials in your field. The benchmarks you set for yourself can force you to improve your level of performance and avoid settling onto a plateau of activity that brings boredom. Without this constant exercise, you might think you are making progress when you really aren't becoming what you want to be. On the other hand, you might begin to have stirrings of discontent when an honest appraisal would show that you are in the right place or headed there.

Managers can feel free today to determine their own benchmarks. They discuss career aspirations with bosses, family, and friends to determine which goals are realistic, how they fit into the organization's needs, and how their supervisors can help in the development process. They then begin their planning by answering some down-to-earth questions. What would I like to learn to do well? What would I like to quit doing? What new things would I like to start doing right away? What sort of daily routine would I like to follow? Do I work better in an atmosphere of freedom or under close supervision?

A manager should know whether he wants to continue learning in detail about his specialty or be exposed to new fields. He must decide whether the fine points or the big picture are more interesting. A determined person then seeks certain projects, educational experiences, or totally new jobs that will build his expertise. Today, a manager lets it be known that he wants a certain type of experience and will change companies, if necessary, to get it. He may even take a step backwards for a short time. More than one manager has taken what looks like a demotion to cross functional lines into a new area. Strengthening weak areas helps develop a person into the broad-gauged type of manager who is needed at the higher levels. However, that does not apply to the person who is set on being a top-flight specialist; that person needs to concentrate on building upon his strengths.

TOOTING YOUR OWN HORN

In addition to the planning and development they engage in to work toward what they want to be, managers feel they can generally call attention to themselves in order to win recognition and to improve their chances for motion along the path they have set for themselves. Along with the professionalism of managers has come a higher level and a broader range of expectations. And, like most Americans, they demand prompt reward for accomplishment.

When upper management fails to provide recognition, successful managers trumpet their ideas and accomplishments. Performance and potential may get you to where you want to be, but they won't always do it alone. The right people may not be aware of what you have to offer and what you want. You can make a favorable impression by making your ambitions known, so long as you don't "toot the horn" too often or too loudly.

Top managers can offer a variety of suggestions on how ambitious managers can, over the long haul, build the kind of image that will help them get to where they want to be. But these successful managers generally scoff at the notion that a short-term campaign can influence a promotion decision. It is more likely, they suggest, that short-term tactics will irreparably damage a career. In politics, it's possible to divert attention from a lackluster performance in the office with an image-building campaign. In business, people take a hard look at performance; they don't want to work with a loser.

A campaign might be something as inoffensive as asking to be considered for a job that represents a switch from the normal progression within the company. For positions of major responsibility, most companies try to have the next persons in line identified at all times since vacancies are inevitable. But when the vacancy comes along, this practice can cause the best qualified, but not obvious, candidate to be overlooked, especially if he or she is somewhere outside the normal line of progression for that position.

There are ways to reinforce a good record with actions that create a positive impression. A middle manager with a large oil company was intrigued by a job opening in another division — one that meant a considerable advance for him. He felt he would have to overcome his lack of familiarity with that division's operations, since many of the candidates for the post were already in the division and better known to those who would be making the selection. "There were about 40 candidates, and the job required some technical expertise, which I had to develop," he recalls. "Therefore, I felt I would have to do more than just send in my application. I wanted to draw enough attention to my credentials to ensure that I would at least get an interview. So I began doing some research on the department that was offering the job — the people, their responsibilities, their objectives. At a week-long seminar, I met one of the department's employees and later called him for background."

After discussing his thoughts with his boss and his boss's boss, this manager spent two weeks putting together a 25-page brochure on himself. In addition to his career history with the company, he included a section on what his objectives would be if he got the new job and how he planned to attain them. He got the job.

When the path to the job you want passes through a different department, the first stop should be your boss's office to announce your ambitions, to explain why you have to move elsewhere to achieve them, and to ask for his or her permission to try for an opening elsewhere. The boss may even offer assistance, or at least prepare a recommendation. Before broadcasting your ambitions, it pays to assess the management climate in the company, however. In a hostile environment, ambition is threatening. Even where ambition is appreciated, sharing your plans works only if it does not look like you're out to win at any cost.

Executing personal career plans requires sensitivity to the boss and to others who will be affected by your attempts to gain recognition. It pays to make sure, too, that what you regard as good work is the sort of thing for which your boss will give recognition. If, you have a boss who likes people to meet deadlines, you won't be praised for good work that is late, whereas you might make more points by being on time with less-than-perfect work. It is also important to determine whether you are not, in fact, getting some unspoken recognition. Perhaps the boss's way of giving it is by bestowing difficult assignments on you.

The recognition that is given you does not always come in response to your deliberate attempts to win it. Quite often, for example, when management is sizing up promotion candidates, it looks at some of the subtle signs of interest and disinterest. Some people reveal their ability to accept more responsibility by their behavior in their present work. A manager can win a reputation that will last a long time by digging in on a major project or by attacking a special problem. The reverse is also true. Despite any lofty ambitions, a manager may reveal the lack of genuine interest in greater responsibilities by coasting through a critical project without applying the extra effort called for.

In the entry level ranks, promotions are expected by both the employee and by management. However, as people rise through the management ranks, seldom will the boss walk into a manager's office and announce that he or she is under consideration for promotion. More likely, says one senior manager, "You could be on the golf course, at lunch, or at a party, and someone will ask you what you think about Chicago or the company's operation in Tulsa. And you say the place is rotten or that the job is one you're glad you don't have. Brother, you may have just turned down a promotion."

TURNING DOWN A PROMOTION

Some of the signals given by people regarding their promotability are not so silent. In recent years, many managers have deliberately declined promotions offered to them. If the next job up the line doesn't fit their lifestyles, they don't view it as a promotion.

"His wife hates the company; they have moved 12 times in the last 17 years. The kids are miserable in their new home. But . . . . that was the next step up for him. What could he do?" So went the talk among the neighborhood wives when Dick got his latest promotion.

For every job, it seems there is a "what comes next?" We have long assumed that each position is essentially a rung on the ladder — not something in itself. People are beginning to rebel against the notion that they must climb the ladder that takes them away from the lifestyles they want. No one knows for sure what will happen if a manager declines a promotion. Once it was certain career suicide to do so. The risk may be nearly as great as ever, but more people are willing to take it.

Declining a promotion that involves a transfer to another location is generally excusable but only for the short term — "until the kids are out of school," or "until my health improves," for example.

Most companies understand such reasons and will not cross a manager's name off their future promotion list. But once they can no longer see a special circumstance, you either accept the offer or resign yourself to staying where you are indefinitely. At least, that's the way it has been up to now. As refusals proliferate, management will have to pay greater attention to personal wants. This has been the case with rehiring people who previously left the company. Company policy used to dictate that once you quit, the door was forever closed to you; today, few companies will turn down a good applicant who once worked there. In fact, some keep close tabs on the whereabouts of former key people, in the hopes of hiring them back someday.

Reasons for turning down a promotion in terms of the work itself range from feeling that the offer simply isn't a step upward to fearing that it is too much of a step. A "promotion" is in the eyes of the beholder. If the boss thinks a change is a promotion and you don't, it's not a promotion for you. Or, if you think it's a promotion and find satisfaction in the new job, who cares what the rest of the world thinks? More and more managers feel it isn't a promotion if it doesn't take you where you want to be — if the kinds of responsibility, the functional area, the job routine, or the surrounding lifestyle don't match your wants.

Some managers decline promotions, rightly or wrongly, because they feel they have reached their maximum level of performance. They feel they have mastered their profession or specialty and have no desire to accept the challenge to develop new skills. Management will sometimes accept this reasoning. If a person is competent in his current job and rejecting the advancement won't affect performance, they often prefer to leave him where he is. They believe a happy, productive employee is better than one forced into frustration and ineffectiveness.

A major category of reasons for declining a promotion — especially if it involves a relocation to another geographic area — is family considerations. Employee Transfer Corporation, in a survey of 300 persons who had been transferred, found in 1979 that 71 percent considered the transfer stressful. More than a third reported that a member of their family had noticeably changed in attitude or behavior since the transfer. Most frequently, their children were troubled by uprooted friendships or school problems. Ironically, 20 percent said the transfer was not necessary for their advancement, and 30 percent received no increase in pay. But 31 percent say they felt forced to accept the transfer.

Part of the sizing up of candidates should include an evaluation of whether the promotion suits the individual from his or her point of view. Management risks causing some disappointments by tipping off too many people that they are under consideration for a promotion. The best way to ease around this possibility is to have developed this information in routine conversations or periodic performance appraisals when conversation about career goals can be dealt with in general terms rather than in relation to a specific opening.

Although top corporate people generally are not inclined to take punitive action against anyone who rejects a promotion, they admit that turning down a promotion is tantamount to telling them that they made a mistake in selection. Since few senior managers like to be told they are wrong, it is better to have made your interests known early in the game.

Today, managers have the choice to use the mobility that is available to them or to decline to use it. A young manager may shake his head in silence while listening to a middle-aged manager boast of his many transfers over the years. Some managers seem unaware that they have put their career goals above all other considerations. But younger managers have been sensitized to the sacrifice of self and family.

Some managers grow and fulfill themselves as they move about; some do not. Some of their children adapt and broaden as they move about the country; others withdraw and pay the price of a parent's "success." The mechanisms for mobility are in place, but people are going to use them only as they alone choose.

STAYING TURNED ON

Ladders of progression and the definition of success that accompanies them are designed to stimulate activity. People who refuse to be forced into "progress" that they don't want have to guard that they are not simply dropping out. They have to demonstrate that they are internally motivated and working toward something that is more important to them.

Working with intangibles, managers are especially likely to feel from time to time that they are not accomplishing anything. One corporate chairman says the best way to overcome this feeling is to take a fresh approach to your present job. "There isn't a job anywhere that can't be done better than it is presently being done. Psych yourself up by sitting down and thinking through what you want to accomplish over the next two years or so. Then make a list of what you have to do and set a timetable. All of a sudden, you realize you're behind schedule and you'd better get at it."

If you are where you thought you wanted to be and you still aren't getting the satisfaction and identity you want from your work, you can do several things to get yourself turned on again:

- Take stock of your accomplishments and shortcomings.
- Review that career plan, reassessing yourself and your goals.
- Delegate more activities and go on to more challenging tasks.
- Look for broadening projects, special assignments, or training.
- Plot a course to a new target.

People build their careers on hope — hope of accomplishment, hope of greater income, hope of power, hope of recognition. At some point, they are likely to be overwhelmed with the question: "What have I done with my life?" In order to avoid setting themselves up for regrets and doubts, successful managers try to plan their lives to attain success in broader dimensions than those permitted on an organization chart. They refuse to segment their lives into meaningless pieces and sell the largest chunk for a paycheck.

While some managers have surrendered themselves to the system and others have taken all they could get from it, a manager now has the opportunity to work the system to mutual advantage. It is this type who stands to gain most from the system and to provide the leadership for the future. People are convinced that there is more to life than work and more to work than a paycheck; they will be led by managers who share that belief. Therefore, as managers become what they want to be, the corporation will become what it has to be.

THE POWER OF THE PERSON

What the corporation finds at its doors now is a potential management corps of accomplishers rather than careerists — people who are seeking accomplishment for themselves and for their organizations. Although they reject the win/lose proposition offered by the traditional corporate hierarchy, they are willing to share objectives that they consider worthwhile. They are not mobilizing a revolution against the corporation, but they are expressing attitudes to which the corporation must respond and from which it can benefit.

Managers themselves will be the pivot in the turn to humanagement in the future corporation. Imposing personal expectations on the organization, they will open the doors to diversity and individuality. Because our society has become so diverse, it must either be constrained by autocrats or led to consensus by humanistic managers. It will be up to the manager of the future to ensure that the revolution in the workplace does not become a matter of worker versus manager or individual versus system.

A closeness has been developing between worker and manager in the American corporate system, especially since the great democratization effect of World War II. Yet, there has been a holding back, to varying degrees, of the manager's own humanity and his or her recognition of the humanity of others. But this withholding is becoming a detriment to effectiveness and satisfaction for all concerned. The progression to humanagement will remove that needless limitation on the power of the individual. Humanagement will support people's efforts to personalize the system of which they are a part. It will provide an alternative to the path taken in other industrialized nations, where worker ownership or government ownership have become poor substitutes for people's genuine, personal involvement in their work and for corporate responsiveness to society's needs.

People organized to fulfill dreams for themselves and their society will be a far more potent force than those who are servants to routine. The corporation will improve in effectiveness and relevance, not by change in structure or ownership, but by change in attitude. It will become more participative. This does not mean, however, that it will become some sort of democracy. People will be encouraged to offer their inputs, but decisions will not be left to majority rule. They will, instead, be put in the hands of those special people who can deal with values and feelings as well as systems and facts. People will continue to make sacrifices — a necessity for being a member of any group — but they will have a better chance to belong, contribute, grow, and support themselves economically. They stand now on the threshold of attaining both material and psychic rewards from their work.

As the corporation becomes more dedicated to the quality of life in everything it does, it will depend on managers who are whole people. Given the freedom to be what he or she wants to be, a manager is more likely to feel like a whole person while serving the organization. Both the individual manager and the corporation will benefit, since the person whose life makes sense is best prepared to manage complexity.

Chapter Notes

The following sources of quotations and examples are articles published in *Industry Week* unless otherwise indicated.

CHAPTER 1

Frederick Herzberg, "Putting people back together," July 24, 1978.
John S. Mc Clenahen, "Rockwell's Jeffs seeks 'space' for people," August 7, 1978.
Perry Pascarella, "Humanagement," May 14, 1979.
Daniel Yankelovich, "We need new motivational tools," August 6, 1979.
"High achieving managers called 'open, communicative, people-oriented' by five-year teleometrics project," *World of Work Report*, Work in America Institute, Volume 4, Number 2, February 1979.

CHAPTER 2

Charles Day Jr., "Youth at the top," May 9, 1977.
Charles Day Jr., "Corporate monarchs losing grip?" February 20, 1978.
Charles Day Jr., "The race women haven't won," April 2, 1979.
Golightly & Co. International, Inc., Study on chief executive officer backgrounds, 1977.
Michael L. Johnson, "The young manager: where is he taking industry?" January 6, 1975.

Michael L. Johnson, "Women: Born to manage," August 4, 1975.

Reginald H. Jones, chairman, General Electric Co., Speech to New York Chamber of Commerce and Industry, "Meeting the future unsurprised," September 21, 1977.

Brian S. Moskal, "Management striving for sexual detente," March 5, 1979.

Perry Pascarella and Daniel D. Cook, "Can you win?" January 23, 1978.

"Renaissance man . . . Back in a business suit," May 4, 1970.

CHAPTER 3

Daniel D. Cook, "A convert labors in the lion's den," March 20, 1978.

Michael L. Johnson, "How managers 'farm' their careers," April 19, 1976.

Brian S. Moskal, "The great M.B.A. talent hunt," October 16, 1978.

Marilyn Much, "Few firms offer the ultimate 'perk,' " November 13, 1978.

Perry Pascarella, "Am I falling behind?" September 15, 1975.

Perry Pascarella, "What's going on around here?" September 29, 1975.

CHAPTER 4

Charles Day Jr., "What it takes to be a CEO," January 8, 1979.

Roger Gould, Special interview, February 1979.

Perry Pascarella, "What makes a good manager?" September 1, 1975.

John H. Sheridan, "Staying on course through the takeover gauntlet," September 4, 1978.

John H. Sheridan, "Is there still room for bold managers?" December 5, 1977.

Ross Whitehead, "Emotion can make, or break, a manager," March 6, 1978.

CHAPTER 5

Fred T. Allen, "Corporate ethics; a view from the top," April 11, 1977.

Daniel D. Cook, "What worries managers most," May 1, 1978.

Charles Day Jr., "Complying with regulators demands new 'steering' skills," October 24, 1977.

Floyd G. Lawrence, "Whose ethics guide business?" October 27, 1975.

John H. Sheridan, "Can your job put you in jeopardy?" May 31, 1976.

Donald B. Thompson, "Runaway regulation drains management spirit," August 15, 1977.

Daniel Yankelovich, "Managing in an age of anxiety," October 24, 1977.

CHAPTER 6

Charles Day Jr., "Things they didn't tell me about the new job," July 18, 1977.

Charles Day Jr., "Management's mindless mistakes," May 29, 1978.

John S. McClenahen, "FMC's Malott spreads executive power," October 10, 1977.

Perry Pascarella, "Am I an 'us' or a 'them'?" September 8, 1975.

Donald B. Thompson, "Many fail management's sternest test," March 19, 1979.

"Managing, meddling, or monkeying around," May 17, 1971.

"Mistakes managers make," August 23, 1971.

"Why some young execs go astray," November 22, 1971.

CHAPTER 7

William M. Ellinghaus, Remarks at Work in America conference, sponsored by Work in America Institute, March 14, 1979.

Charles A. Nekvasil, "You're the leader, but will they follow?" November 18, 1974.

Perry Pascarella, "What's the best management style?" October 6, 1975.

John H. Sheridan, "Do more, work less," April 17, 1978.
"Japanese management style wins converts," April 16, 1979.
"Toughest job of all — delegating," January 25, 1971.

CHAPTER 8

Donald R. Long, "Tearing down departmental walls," July 30, 1973.
Marilyn Much, "Company structures respond to change," August 2, 1976.
Donald B. Thompson, "The ultimate 'word': The grapevine," May 10. 1976.
"Organizations: Tops, bottoms, and turmoil," May 4, 1970.
"How to survive in the corporate jungle," November 15, 1971.
"Surviving the power struggle," August 2, 1976.

CHAPTER 9

Stephen H. Fuller, Remarks at Managing Human Resources conference, sponsored by The Conference Board, March 15, 1979.
Richard F. Gibson, "Discipline: Search for new solutions," July 15, 1974.
Louis Harris, Remarks at Working in the Twenty-first Century Conference, April 3–4, 1979.
James H. Jordan, Remarks at Working in the Twenty-first Century Conference, April 3–4, 1979.
Perry Pascarella, "Are Charlie's troubles my business?" September 22, 1975.
Vivian C. Pospisil, "Should you pull strings for the young manager?" September 26, 1977.
Thomas M. Rohan, "Grooming the heir apparent," September 18, 1978.
Jerome M. Rosow, Remarks at Working in the Twenty-first Century conference, April 3–4, 1979.
Florence R. Skelly, Remarks at Managing Human Resources conference, sponsored by the Conference Board, March 15, 1979.
Donald B. Thompson, "Profit from the wisdom in your shop," February 14, 1977.

Michael A. Verespej, "Boss, I have a great idea," February 2, 1976.
"How to fire an executive," May 31, 1971.
"Discipline: Laying down the law – productively," May 17, 1976.

CHAPTER 10

Michael L. Johnson, "Conquering clocks and calendars," April 12, 1976.
Michael L. Johnson, "Coping with 'executive extras,'" April 26, 1976.
Perry Pascarella, "How can I keep the boss happy?" October 13, 1975.
Perry Pascarella, "When you have a dynamic follower," September 26, 1977.
"How the pro manages himself," January 26, 1970.
"Support your boss to advantage – yours and his," October 18, 1971.
"How to break the routine," November 29, 1971.
"Can you finish by sundown?" April 17, 1972.
"Remember that the boss is human, too," October 29, 1973.

CHAPTER 11

Daniel D. Cook, "Are you a prisoner of your industry?" February 19, 1979.
Charles Day Jr., "Is job loyalty a worthless virtue?" August 21, 1978.
Roger Gould, Special interview, February 1979.
Frederick Herzberg, "Careerists, accomplishers, and the obsolete," August 21, 1978.
Lad Kuzela, "What it's like to bargain for millions," June 6, 1977.
Floyd G. Lawrence, "Middle managers voice their discontent," September 6, 1976.
William H. Miller, "Miseries of the misfit managers," April 16, 1979.
Brian S. Moskal, "Executive life-styles: Shifting priorities," February 6, 1978.
Perry Pascarella, "How we waste management talent," April 23, 1973.

Vivian C. Pospisil, "Problems of dual-career marriages," November 15, 1976.

Margaret Price, "Wedding vows a career must?" January 22, 1979.

Michael A. Verespej, "Young tigers revisited," July 24, 1978.

Michael A. Verespej, "The entertaining executive: Fun by objectives," November 13, 1978.

"Is the grass really greener?" January 12, 1970.

"Why managers drift away," April 6, 1970.

"Corporate wife: The loneliest job in town," April 29, 1974.

"The company and the executive wife," August 26, 1974.

"Transferred wives: The other side of 'success,' " February 28, 1977.

"Profile of a winner – Knight," October 30, 1978.

CHAPTER 12

Michael L. Johnson, "Plan your career or wing it?" September 30, 1974.

John J. Mullally, "Is it un-American to turn down a promotion?" December 6, 1976.

John H. Sheridan, "Campaigning for a promotion," May 9, 1977.

John H. Sheridan, "Would you want your child to be a manager?" October 2, 1978.

"The blues at 50," November 1, 1976.

"Results of annual transferee attitude survey," *Moving Picture*, Employee Transfer Corp., 1979.

Index

Index